The Collected Piano Works of
R. Nathaniel Dett

With Introductions by
Dominique-Rene de Lerma and Vivian Flagg McBrier

Foreword by
ELLIS MARSALIS

Library of Congress Cataloging in Publication Data

Dett, Robert Nathaniel, 1882-1943.
   The collected piano works of R. Nathaniel Dett.

Suites.
Reproduced from the original editions published by
C.F. Summy Co., J. Church Co., and Mills Music.
   CONTENTS: Magnolia. — In the bottoms. — Enchantment. [etc.]

   1. Suites (Piano)
M24.D333   786.1'092'4   72-12872
ISBN 0-87487-080-1

Summy-Birchard Inc.
exclusively distributed by
Warner Bros. Publications
15800 NW 48th Avenue
Miami, FL 33014

Contents

R. Nathaniel Dett

My initial introduction to the piano music of Dett came about forty-five years ago. My piano teacher, Jean Coston Maloney, assigned a piece to me from his *In the Bottoms* suite. The piece was *DANCE* (Juba).

At the time, my musical interest was elsewhere and I continue to regret until today my inability to discipline myself to prepare this piece to recital readiness. A genuine appreciation of Dett's music would come later in my life; well beyond the teen years of my studies with Maloney.

When listening to Dett's piano music it is immediately obvious that he made a conscious decision to dedicate his life to composing music influenced by Spirituals sung by Negro slaves in the southern regions of North America. A Canadian by birth, these songs were sung to him as a child by his grandmother and would have a lasting effect on his creative spirit.

In his approach to composition, Dett would embrace both the sacred as well as secular lifestyle of his ancestral legacy. From his *In the Bottoms* suite, the somber texture of *Prelude* and the ebullient impressionism of *Dance* reflect Dett's concept of both sacred and secular views of American-African community life.

This music is not "Classical" in the Eurocentric sense of the word. However, Dett's formal study of Western music enhanced his compositional techniques in both the instrumental and vocal arenas. This collection for pianoforte illustrates a group of short pieces that give us a glimpse of America from Dett's perspective of the first half of the twentieth century.

Unlike its renegade offspring Jazz, the Negro Spirituals represented, in Detts' words "the best class of Negro music." When asked by Carl Engel, Chief of the Music Division at the Library of Congress, to accept a commission to compose a piece for an instrumentation that included saxophone and banjo, obviously Jazz related instruments, Dett considered his request an affront. While not wishing to reject a commission, Dett tried to circumvent the designated instrumentation and Engel's request for a work with "a distinctly racial flavor."

Justifying his position Dett would invoke the disapproval by the Negro church of the banjo and the saxophone as reasons for reaction. He would go even further citing the saxophone and the banjo as "instruments of the devil." Even though Engel relented in the original guidelines for the commission, there is no evidence that Dett relented his stance. We can only lament through speculation what we have missed by his decision or indecision, as the case may be, regarding the Engel proposal.

In *The Collected Piano Works of R. Nathaniel Dett*, we have a wonderful group of pieces that can inject a unique musical flavor when performed on a recital of longer works of Beethoven, Chopin, Liszt, or the equally short preludes of Debussy. Pianists who perform American music would do well to include some of these pieces in public recitals, studio recitals and various piano competitions.

As we approach the twenty-first century with its myriad technological devices competing for the minds of our youth, the challenge to the teachers of the pianoforte requires a renewed dedication. The piano music of twentieth century American-African composers presents a unique opportunity for a more comprehensive approach to a much needed endeavor; continuing the art of pianoforte playing as well as performing the previously ignored compositions of non-European composers. *The Collected Piano Works of R. Nathaniel Dett* is an excellent choice for the twenty-first century piano pedagogues and performers.

Ellis L. Marsalis, Jr.
Director of Jazz Studies Division
University of New Orleans

The Man

Robert Nathaniel Dett was born October 11, 1882, in Drummondsville, Ontario, a city about sixty miles north of the Vermont border, which was largely populated by former slaves and their families. His mother, too, was born in Canada, at Niagara Falls, but otherwise his ancestors came from the United States. His father, Robert Tue Dett, had been employed in railroad service and was owner of a hotel in Niagara Falls, New York. Nathaniel had two brothers, Samuel W. Dett, the oldest of the children, and Arthur Newton Dett, the second oldest, who was fatally shot in a child-hood accident. One sister, Harriett (named for her grandmother), died at the age of two.

Young Nathaniel visited the piano lessons of his brothers. When Mrs. Marshall, their teacher, was out of the room, he would play his brothers' pieces. Because of this display of talent, the family arranged for Mrs. Marshall to give Nathaniel lessons also. After the Detts moved to their hotel in Niagara Falls, they engaged John Weiss to instruct the boy.

By the time Nathaniel was fourteen, he had a part-time job as a bellhop at the Cataract Hotel in Niagara Falls and also played the piano at church. From 1901 to 1903 he studied at the Oliver Willis Halstead Conservatory in nearby Lockport, then enrolled at Oberlin Conservatory of Music in 1903. Here he studied piano with Howard Handel Carter and George Carl Hastings, organ with J.R. Frampton and G.W. Andrews, voice with J.W. Horner, theory with A.E. Heacox and F. Lehman, composition with G.W. Andrews, and music history with Edward Dickinson. During the years at Oberlin (1903-1908), he gained initial experience as a choral director in a local church. A performance at Oberlin by the Kneisel String Quartet of "a slow movement by Dvorak based on traditional airs" (most likely the "American" Quartet, Op. 96) had a profound effect on Dett. This work, which reflects the great interest Dvorak had in Black-American music, reminded Dett of the spirituals his grandmother had sung to him in his youth. Spirituals were not then popular with Blacks because they were a reminder of slavery days. Nevertheless, Dett resolved to dedicate his life to the preservation and advancement of this music.

In 1908 Dett graduated from Oberlin, the first Black to earn the Bachelor of Music degree with a major in composition and piano — a five-year course. He was then engaged as piano teacher and conductor of the Lane Choral Society at Lane College in Jackson, Tennessee.

In 1910 he was offered a teaching position with the Kansas City high school but did not accept. The next year, following a recital tour which took him to Memphis, Birmingham, Mason City, and Alabama State College, he joined the faculty of the Lincoln Institute (now University) in Jefferson City, Missouri. This post paid three times as much as his previous teaching appointment.

In 1913 Dett was engaged by Hampton Institute. Despite this important position, he spent the summer at Oberlin in study with Karl Gehrkens. His interest in additional education occupied much of his non-teaching time for the next twenty years.

His most popular work, *In the Bottoms*, was published in 1913 by Clayton F. Summy and given its premiere in Chicago by Fanny Bloomfield-Zeisler, a distinguished concert pianist of the day. Percy Grainger, another well-known pianist, programmed this suite many times and helped make it popular.

Two concerts in 1914 contributed to Dett's standing as composer and pianist. The first, presented in league with Harry T. Burleigh at the Samuel Coleridge-Taylor Club, included Dett's *Magnolia*; the second was an "All Colored Composers' Concert," presented in Chicago on June 3. In addition to Dett's *Magnolia* and *In the Bottoms*, works by Coleridge-Taylor, Burleigh, J. Rosamond Johnson, and Will Marion Cook were performed. Karleton Hackett in the *Chicago Evening Post* (June 4, 1914) gave Dett's piano suites the best notice. Felix Borowski, another reviewer, was in agreement: "We believe that his abilities are such as to qualify him for the leader-ship of the musical creators among his people [Dett's] ideas ... are often distinguished for originality." Borowski also had high praise for Dett's piano performance.

In the summer of 1915 Dett studied under Peter Dykema at Columbia University, then attended classes at the American Conservatory in Chicago and at Northwestern University.

The major event of 1916 was his marriage to Helen Elise Smith on December 27, at St. Philip's Church in New York. His bride was the first Black graduate of the Damrosch Institute of Musical Art (absorbed in 1926 by the Juilliard School of Music). She had been a student of Sigismond Stojowski and Percy Goetschius, and her performance as pianist had been warmly praised by Henry Krehbiel. Following her graduation, she served as a director of the Martin Smith

School of Music in New York, and was associated with the Music Settlement School for Colored People. Two daughters came from this union: Helen, born in 1918, and Josephine Elizabeth, born in 1922.

Dett spend 1920 at Harvard University as a student of Arthur Foote. While there he won the Francis Boott Prize for his setting of "Don't Be Weary Traveler" and the Bowdoin Prize for his essay *The Emancipation of Negro Music*.

National recognition became particularly evident in 1924 when Dett was honored during Music Week at Niagara Falls, was awarded an honorary doctorate from Howard University, and was elected president of the National Association of Negro Musicians. In 1926 he received a second honorary doctorate, this time from his alma mater Oberlin.

During his years at Hampton, Dett developed the Hampton Institute Choir, which made an extraordinary impression on its tours and was invited to participate in a concert at the Library of Congress in 1926. In a letter concerning the preliminary arrangements for this concert, Carl Engel, Chief of the Music Division, made a proposal which stimulated Dett to reveal his cultural integrity. "I am anxious to know," Engel wrote "if you would be interested in accepting the commission to write a quartet for the following instruments: piano, violin, saxophone, and banjo. The work would be in the form of a suite, or in the regular quartet form of three or four movements. But personally, I should think that a suite of three movements would be the happier form, as it would not be too long, and yet afford enough change for effective contrasts between the various movements. I purposely refrain from using the word 'jazz' in connection with such a work, but I have in mind that the work should have a distinctly racial flavor and yet be in the truest sense first-class chamber music." Funding for the project was to come from Elizabeth Sprague Coolidge, a major figure in American chamber music, who had been deeply impressed with Dett's work at Hampton and who was the sponsor for the Library of Congress concert scheduled for later that year.

Dett replied: "I am going to be very candid with you. All races have inheritances: left to their own devices, they will naturally follow their native bent. An effort from the outside to lay down rather strict lines along which their art should develop can only result in self-consciousness and, consequently, in unartistic and insincere results. If I may be so bold as to make a suggestion, it would be this: that without trying to prescribe for what instruments or combination of instruments any Negro should write, he should be promised a reward for any composition — chamber music if you like — employing an indigenous idiom."

Engel answered that a commission might often state specific instrumentation, and that his suggestion would be in effect a "rehabilitation" for the banjo and the saxophone. "Moreover," Engel added, the ensemble "would have the merit of being a novelty," but then he capitulated and asked that Dett ignore these guidelines.

Dett amplified his ideas. "The instruments you suggested have never been approved by the Negro church as an institution. The fact that the Negro church has dominated Negro life almost entirely would make the use of the instruments which you suggest incongruous to the expression you seem to wish. Do what we will, we cannot run away from the traditions and associations. The best class of Negro music, which is represented by the spirituals, could never in the Negro mind be interpreted on a banjo or a saxophone which, to the bondsman's point of view, were instruments of the devil. Also, the long-draw-out style of the more soulful of Negro songs could not be faithfully portrayed on a banjo, although the saxophone might do this reasonably well; also the associations of the saxophone have not been regarded as respectable, even by people whose racial background is not a religious one. It is evident then, how much more improper such an instrument would be to interpret Negro music truly."

Engel replied: "To be quite frank, it had not occurred to me that in our day 'the Negro church as an institution' would have a deciding influence on the development of Negro music. Nor can I — with perhaps my limited grasp of the situation — conceive of that influence as a particularly fruitful one, at least not so far as a higher type of instrumental music is concerned." Engel's understanding of Black music and the Black church was evidently very faulty. There is no evidence the matter was ever discussed again.

Engel subsequently suggested that Dett include on his Library of Congress concert a chain-gang song by Mary Howe, a Washington composer. The conductor regarded the work as being "very original and interesting," but he did not find its spirit in harmony with that which he had designed for the concert. The concert was finally presented on December 17, so well attended that there were not enough programs to satisfy the needs of the audience.

The following year, during which Dett was given the first Harmon award for music, he published *Religious Folk-Songs of the Negro as Sung at Hampton Institute*. In 1928, the School of Music was established at Hampton, and Dett was named director. He also presented a concert at Carnegie Hall with his Choir.

In the summer of 1929 Dett went to Fontainebleau to study with Nadia Boulanger. This distinguished teacher was impressed with Dett's talents but, sensitive to the differences in direction of their musical aims, feared imposing her instruction on his native gifts.

Financed by John D. Rockefeller, George Foster Peabody and others, the Hampton Institute Choir made a concert tour of Europe in 1930. Performing in famous concert halls, they brought Black-American music to European audiences, which included royalty and state officials.

Dett secured a leave of absence from Hampton Institute in 1931 in order to complete work for a Master of Music degree at the Eastman School of Music. There he studied piano with Max Landow and composition with Bernard Rogers and Howard Hanson. His thesis, originally titled *Composition for Chorus and Orchestra*, has since become known as *The Ordering of Moses*. The first performance of this was given by the Cincinnati Symphony in 1937, followed soon after by performances at the Juilliard School of Music and the Westchester Music Festival.

On graduating from Eastman, Dett submitted his resignation to Hampton and stayed on in Rochester for several years. He engaged in private teaching and, starting in 1933, was conductor of a sixteen-voice chorus for Stromberg-Carlson's weekly NBC broadcasts. For the centennial anniversary of the city of Rochester in 1934, Dett was given three weeks to write incidental music to Edward Hungerford's pageants, *Parade of the Years* and *Pathways of Progress*. Also during this year he conducted a chorus of two hundred and fifty in a Washington D.C. concert of his works.

Returning to academic life in 1937, Dett moved to Bennett College in Greensboro, North Carolina, as Visiting Director of Music. This new situation at an all-girl school gave him an impetus for the creation of several works for women's chorus.

In 1940 Dett took his chorus from Bennett on a tour of the United States and Canada, and broadcast over CBS with this group. He served as guest lecturer at Virginia State College and at Northwestern University in 1941. Despite what he was accomplishing, he grew restless and lamented the little time he had for composition. In 1942 he resigned from Bennett, returning to Rochester where he was associated with St. Simon's Episcopal Church.

As early as 1937 Percy Grainger had asked Dett if he would write some music for the high school band at the National Music Camp at Interlochen, but Dett felt he would not be able to accomplish the task properly. His difficulty in working with a large instrumental ensemble, which he rarely attempted, is manifest in the orchestration of *The Ordering of Moses*.

Dett continued to maintain correspondence with Grainger and wrote on August 4, 1943: "I regret not being able to have stayed over [in Washington] to have heard your concert at Meridian Hill, but as you know, I have to go where the USO sends me." Dett had become musical advisor to the entertainment organization for the military forces, and had been assigned to Battle Creek in July, where he trained a WAC chorus at Ft. Custer. Perhaps his last work to be completed was the suite *Bible Vignettes*, which he wanted to send to Grainger. Dett's health suddenly failed and on October 2, he succumbed to a heart attack. He was buried at Fairview Cemetery in Niagara Falls, Ontario.

Dett was not a composer of highest rank when considering extended forms (his *Ordering of Moses* is a work of great merit but of distinctly uneven quality). His most successful works appear to be his choral works based on Negro spirituals and his suites for piano. As perhaps with Beethoven, harmonic inventiveness and exploration of texture and form appear most strongly in Dett's music for piano. From his piano writing it is evident he had substantial keyboard technique. Most important in his life, however, was the dedication of his talents to the cause of the music of his people. As an educator, Dett discovered and nurtured the gifts of many persons; as a choral conductor, he gave both Europe and America additional reason to respect the unique musical heritage of Afro-Americans.

I wish to acknowledge my gratitude to those who helped in gathering material for this article, including Prof. Kenneth B. Billups (St. Louis), Howard Brucker (Voice of America), Jean Bowen (New York Public Library), Dr. Ruth Watanabe (Eastman School of Music), Mary M. Rossbach (Oberlin College), Dr. William Grant Still (Los Angeles), Carroll D. Wade and William Lichtenwanger (Library of Congress), Dr. Geneva H. Southall (University of Minnesota), Profs. Maurice McCall, Charles E. Flax, and Irene Saunders (Hampton Institute).

Dominique-René de Lerma
Director, Black Music Center, Indiana University

8

Bibliography

de Lerma, Dominique-René

> *Black Music; A Preliminary Register of the Composers and Their Works.* To be issued in the near future by the Kent State University Press.
>
> *"Dett, Robert Nathaniel"* to appear in the forthcoming supplementary volume of *Die Musik in Geschichte und Gegenwart,* ed. by Friedrich Blume. Kassel: Bärenreiter-Verlag.
>
> *"Dett and Engel: A Question of Cultural Pride"* in *Your musical cue* (Bloomington, Ind.) v7n2 (November 1970) p. 3-5.

Dett, Robert Nathaniel

> *Album of a Heart.* Jackson, Tenn.: Mocowat-Mercer, 1911.
>
> *The Development of the Negro Spiritual.* Minneapolis: Schmitt, Hall & McCreary, 1936.
>
> *"The Emancipation of Negro Music"* in *The Southern Workman* (Hampton) v47 (1918) p172-176.
>
> *"From Bell Stand to Throne Room"* in *Etude* (Philadelphia) v52 (February 1934) p79.
>
> *"Negro Music of the Present"* in *The Southern Workman* (Hampton) v47 (1918) p243-247.

McBrier, Vivian Flagg

> *The Life and Works of Robert Nathaniel Dett.* Dissertation (Ph.D.) Catholic University of America. 1967. Ann Arbor: University Microfilms, 1967 (no. 67-17142).

Pope, Marguerite

> *A Brief Biography of Dr. Robert Nathaniel Dett.* Hampton: Hampton Institute Press, 1945 (also in *Hampton Bulletin,* v42, October 1945).

The Piano Music

It is not surprising that Dett wrote with skill for the piano, as he was a pianist of unusual talent who understood well the mechanical structure of the instrument and the technical possibilities of the performer.

Dett's talent for the piano was evidenced at a very young age. He stated: "I played the piano ever since I can remember; no one taught me, I just picked it up.... I learned to play by listening to my mother." In spite of his formal training, which began at about age seven, Dett was always changing a composition "to make it sound better."

Dett successfully concertized, composed, and taught after graduating from Oberlin Conservatory. That he was a highly respected pianist as well as composer may be seen from the following reviews.

Negro Composer at Orchestra Hall

... Mr. Dett is a pianist of distinct quality and his music had an individual note of charm. It was not pretentious, did not seek to carry any deep message, nor make a propaganda but was content to express with simplicity and intuitive feeling something of the Southland. It was not so folksong like as we had expected with little attempt for racial tone color, but the reflex of an individual to whom the things had personal meaning. There was melodic feeling, graceful rhythmic form, and played with an appreciation that made them delightful. (Karleton Hackett, *Chicago Evening Post* June 13, 1914).

Negro Composer-Pianist Gives Beautiful Recital at Fisk Chapel.

.. Applause is a variable entity. Sometimes it is sympathetic. Sometimes, very often indeed it is perfunctory, and then it is honestly appreciative. But the determined applause that compelled Mr. Dett to halt the trend of his *Magnolia Suite* to repeat that unspeakably soulful poem — without words, "Mammy," was proof conclusion that his hearers had had an experience of rare beauty. (Geo. Pullen Jackson, *Nashville Banner* [Nashville, Tenn.], Feb. 27, 1923).

Negro Composer in Recital of Works

As a pianist, Dett ranks high, playing with ease, often with brilliance, and with a melting pianissimo which makes his heavier passages stand out boldly. (Edna Coates, *Chester* [Pa.] *Times*, Nov. 21, 1931).

The earliest published piano works by Dett are "After the Cake Walk" (1900), "Cave of the Winds" (1902), and "Inspiration Waltzes" (1903). "After the Cake Walk" includes a two-step and polka, as well as a cake walk. "Cave of the Winds" is a vigorous march which uses simple traditional harmony. "Inspiration Waltzes" has a catchy lilting melody and, like "Cave of the Winds," reflects youthful verve. The young composer wrote the following program for "Inspiration Waltzes":

I awoke one night at midnight and heard, as in a dream, the melodies of this Waltz played over and over, until I again fell asleep. Next morning I found it was still fresh in my memory. I created the Introduction and some other parts to give the whole completeness, but the main themes were truly "Inspirations" or, to put it more poetically were truly "dictated by the Muse."

All three of these earliest works represent conventional program music in nineteenth-century style.

In order fully to appreciate the piano music of R. Nathaniel Dett, it must be understood that he was a true Romanticist. Music to him was an expression of the human soul with all of its subjectivism. It was an expression of hope, love, despair; an instrument for his dreams and poetic longings; a vehicle for his racial messages and love for humanity. Dett was a Romantic in both ideological and technical character. All of his piano compositions are programmatic, expressing a racial trait, nature, or a philosophical idea; and most of the compositions are constructed in song-form. His serious published piano compositions may be loosely divided into three periods:

Period I

Magnolia: Suite for Piano (1912)
    Magnolias
    The Deserted Cabin
    To My Lady Love
    Mammy
    The Place Where the Rainbow Ends

In the Bottoms: Characteristic Suite for the Piano (1913)
    Prelude
    His Song
    Honey (Humoresque)
    Barcarolle
    Dance (Juba)

Period II

Enchantment: A Romantic Suite for the Piano on an Original Program (1922)
    Incantation
    Song of the Shrine
    Dance of Desire
    Beyond the Dream

Cinnamon Grove: A Suite for the Piano (1928)
    I. Moderato molto grazioso
    II. Adagio cantabile
    III. Ritmo moderato e con sentimento;
        Quasi Gavotte
    IV. Allegretto

Period III

Tropic Winter: Suite for Piano (1938)
    The Daybreak Charioteer
    A Bayou Garden
    Pompons and Fans
    Legend of the Atoll
    To a Closed Casement
    Noon Siesta
    Parade of the Jasmine Banners

Eight Bible Vignettes
    Father Abraham (1941)
    Desert Interlude (1942)
    As His Own Soul (1942)
    Martha Complained (1942)
    I Am the True Vine (1943)
    Other Sheep (1943)
    Barcarolle of Tears (1943)
    Madrigal Divine (1943)

Dett's first sojourn in the South was at Lane College, Jackson, Tennessee. It is obvious that he was greatly impressed by the beauty of this campus, which is located on a high hill in a little town in southern Tennessee. His first suite bears the title *Magnolia*, showing his love for the beautiful magnolia trees which may still be found on the campus. Each of the five pieces in the suite is descriptive music that portrays Dett's love for nature or pictures the life of the Negro in the South.

The composer gives a detailed program for each of the five compositions in *In the Bottoms*, emphasizing the unifying rhythmic figure and the Negro characteristics.

The compositions of his first period are distinguished by their lyrical melodies, simple structures, and unpretentious charm. The occasional use of syncopation and open fourths and fifths is strongly suggestive of Negro folk-idioms.

The second period includes *Enchantment* and *Cinnamon Grove*. *Enchantment* was dedicated to Percy Grainger, who expressed gratitude for the dedication as "a great honor and kindness." The program to the suite, philosophic in thought and poetic in expression, was written by Dett, who was known as an amateur poet. Grainger referred to the advance in Dett's treatment of harmony and form in this work. There is notable use of chromaticism, altered chords, and ornamentation. It is melodic and has passages which are improvisatory in style.

Cinnamon Grove depends greatly on the literary extra-musical ideas in which Dett shows his great love for and knowledge of poetry, as well as his love for Negro folk song. This suite, too, is highly melodic and chromatic.

Tropic Winter and the *Eight Bible Vignettes* represent the last period of Dett's piano writing. Regarding *Tropic Winter*, Dett wrote to Percy Grainger, "I am proud of this suite, as I think it represents an advance in musical thought..." Among the devices used are chords of the fourth, motivic development, shifting tonalities, altered seventh and ninth chords, and escaped notes.

The *Eight Bible Vignettes* present Dett's love for and knowledge of the Bible. In these eight separate pieces he experiments with structural changes, harmonic devices, and philosophic ideas. As always his melodic lines are distinctive. In "Father Abraham" the Hebrew and Negro melodies are used together effectively. The Hebrew theme is treated contrapuntally with two and three voices answering in free imitation. In "Other Sheep" two classical forms are used: variation and sonata-allegro. "I Am The True Vine" is a tonal three-voiced fugue with a long expressive subject. Throughout the *Vignettes*, Dett uses consecutive fourths and sevenths, augmented, diminished and altered sevenths, and ground bass.

Records show that Dett wrote and performed in concert three unpublished piano compositions: Concert Waltz and Ballade, Sonata in F minor, and Sonate in E minor. Dr. Glenn Dillard Gunn, a Chicago pianist and teacher, stated that in 1919 Dett played a Concert Waltz and Ballade for him, which he found charming and of significant merit. During a 1924 tour, Dett played a Sonata in F minor which was based on original and Negro folk themes. It was well received. The Rockford Illinois *Republic*, February 17, 1925, reported that "The concert [at First Presbyterian Church] opened with a skillful rendition of Dett's own Sonate in E minor, moderato mobile, a composition of considerable musical worth."

It is unfortunate that none of these three works is available, as it is likely that they would add to Dett's stature as a piano composer. Although many of Dett's compositions are gems of beauty, it is regrettable that he did not write in the larger forms, for as he himself said:

Though one who makes pencil sketches on paper may achieve results every bit as perfect in their way as another who chisels similar figures from marble, there is little doubt as to which artist's name will be written higher in the hall of fame.

A study of Dett's piano compositions reveals him not as an innovator, but as a composer with musical sophistication and originality and a scholar with knowledgeable skill. He must be recognized as showing constant growth and development while continuing to maintain and display musical perceptiveness and artistic sensitivity.

He was a Romanticist who composed in small forms and who consistently used extra-musical ideas. His lyrical melodies reflect his deep interest in the voice. He uses the entire keyboard and at times his style seems improvisatory. His compositions are carefully marked with expression and tempo indications, and in difficult passages he often includes helpful fingering.

Dett is a distinguished Black American who wrote well and effectively for the piano and who made a worthy contribution to American music.

Vivian Flagg McBrier
Professor of Music, The District of Columbia Teachers College

Solo Piano Music by R. Nathaniel Dett

After the Cake Walk. Vander Sloot Music Co., 1900.
Bible Vignettes. New York: Mills Music, 1941-1943 (each movement published singly).
Cave of the Winds. Niagara Falls, NY: S.C. Fragard, 1902.
Cinnamon Grove. Cincinnati: J. Church & Co., 1928; pl. no. 19254.
Concert Waltz and Ballade. Unpublished.
Enchantment. Cincinnati: J. Church & Co., 1922; pl. nos. 18540, 18541, 18542, 18543 (each movement published singly).
Fair Weather: a Romantic Suite in the Form of a Sonatine. Unpublished.
In the Bottoms: Chicago: Clayton F. Summy, 1913; pl. no. C.F.S. Co. 1465a-e.
Inspiration Waltzes. New York, London: Richard A. Saalfield, 1903.
Magnolia. Chicago: Clayton F. Summy, 1912, 1922; pl. no. C.F.S. Co. 1387a-b (v. 1, 1387a, contains nos. 1-3; v.2, 1387b, contains nos. 4-5).
Marche Negre. Unpublished. First performed at Hampton, 1915.
My Agnes from Niagara. Niagara Falls, NY: S.C. Fragard, 1909.
Sonate E minor. Performed on 1925 tour. Unpublished.
Sonata F minor. Performed on 1924 tour. Unpublished.
Tropic Winter. Chicago: Clayton F. Summy, 1938; pl. no. C.F. S. Co. 3063a-g.

Publishers Note
No editorial changes have been made in the music other than correction of obvious engravers' errors, such as transposed fingerings, misplaced accidentals, or wrong clefs. We are grateful to Rudolph von Charlton and Mrs. Harriette E. Williamson for supplying copies of missing music, and to Helen Dett Hopkins for her help and cooperation. We also wish to express our deep appreciation to Dr. de Lerma and Dr. McBrier for their interest and dedication in carrying out this project.

MAGNOLIA

Suite for Piano

by R. Nathaniel Dett

CHICAGO

CLAYTON F. SUMMY CO., 64 E. VAN BUREN ST.

WEEKES & CO. LONDON

MAGNOLIA SUITE PART I
No. 1 Magnolias

"Gorgeous Magnolias,
Spotless in splendor,
Sad in their beauty,
Heavy with perfume."

Moderato molto cantabile

No. 2 The Deserted Cabin

Largo con tristezza, melodia ben sostenuto, accomp. stacc.

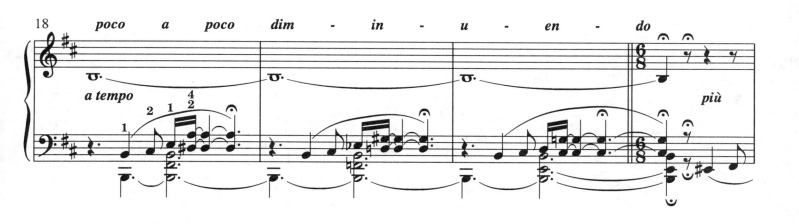

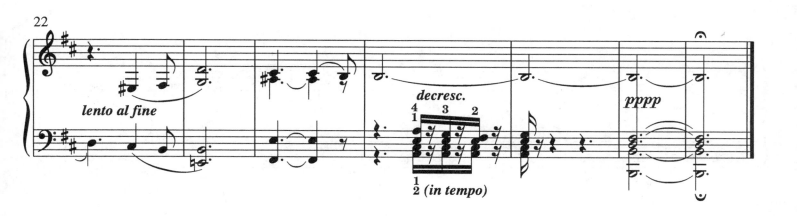

No. 3 My Lady Love

MAGNOLIA SUITE PART II
No. 4 Mammy

No. 5 The Place Where The Rainbow Ends

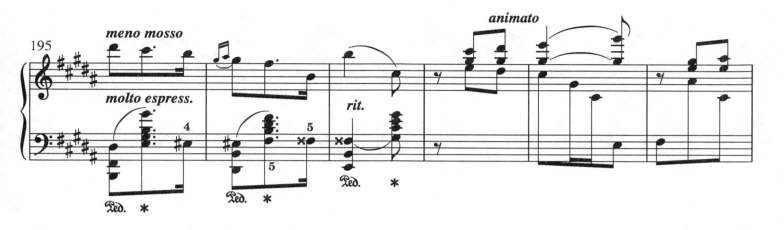

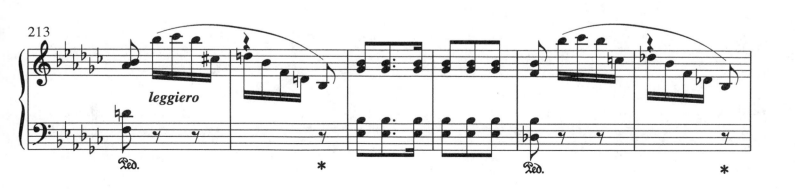

To My Friends The Honourable and Mrs. Fred H. Goff
This Suite Is Gratefully Dedicated

In The Bottoms

CHARACTERISTIC SUITE
FOR THE PIANO
BY
R. Nathaniel Dett

PRELUDE

HIS SONG   BARCAROLLE

HONEY (Humoresque)   DANCE (Juba)

PRICE $1.50

CHICAGO
CLAYTON F. SUMMY CO. 64 E. VAN BUREN ST.
WEEKES & CO. LONDON

IN THE BOTTOMS
Characteristic Suite

"More an expression than a painting."

Beethoven.

"In the Bottoms" is a Suite of five numbers giving pictures of moods or scenes peculiar to Negro life in the river bottoms of the Southern sections of North America. It is similar in its expression, and in a way a continuation of the sentiments already set forth in the "Magnolia" Suite, but suggests ideas incidental to life in a more particular geographic territory. Neither Suite, like Dvořák's famous "New World Symphony" is dependent for its effect upon the introduction of folk songs, either in their natural, or in a highly developed form. As it is quite possible to describe the traits, habits and customs of a people without using the vernacular, so is it similarly possible to musically portray racial peculiarities without the use of national tunes or folk songs. "In the Bottoms," then, belongs to that class of music known as "Program music" or "music with a poetic basis." The source of the "program" or "poetic basis" has already been referred to, and the following notes are appended to show that its relation to the music is intimate.

No. 1. Prelude — is nightfall; the heavy chords represent the heavy shadows, and the open fifths, the peculiar hollow effect of the stillness: the syncopated melody which occurs, is the "tumming" of a banjo, which music is, however, only incidental to the gloom.

No. 2. His Song — The psychological phenomenon is historic, that the moods of suppressed people have oftenest found their most touching expression in song. An aged Negro will sometimes sit for hours in the quiet of an evening, humming an improvised air, whose weird melody seems to strangely satisfy a nameless yearning of the heart.

No. 3. Honey — Literally, "Honey" is a colloquialism — the familiar term of endearment (South). It may mean much, little, everything or nothing; the intimation here, is one of coquetry. It is after a poem, "A Negro Love Song" by Paul Laurence Dunbar.

No. 4. The rhythmic figure, — ♪♪ ♩ — which forms the theme of this Barcarolle is in reality, the rhythmic motif of the whole Suite; it is of most frequent occurrence in the music of the ante-bellum folk-dances, and its marked individuality has caused it to be much misused for purposes of caricature. Here it paints the pleasure of a sunshiny morning on the Father of Waters.

No. 5. Dance — This is probably the most characteristic number of the Suite, as it portrays more of the social life of the people. "Juba" is the stamping on the ground with the foot and following it with two staccato pats of the hands in two-four time. At least one-third of the dancers keep time in this way, while the others dance. Sometimes all will combine together in order to urge on a solo dancer to more frantic (and at the same time more fantastic) endeavors. The orchestra usually consists of a single "fiddler," perched high on a box or table; who, forgetful of self in the rather hilarious excitement of the hour, does the impossible in the way of double stopping and bowing.

*** A word of warning cannot be suppressed in regard to the tempo of the "Dance." Do not take it *too fast!* Much of the dancing in the bottoms is done with a grace and finish that a *Presto* tempo never could suggest.

*** Metronome marks, which should be carefully observed, are given for all of the movements. The Prelude should open and close with an air of mystery, and most of its serenade part be kept subdued as if sounding from afar. Let the major-key portion of His Song have a decidedly hopeful tone as it has prophetic significance. Flirt all you please with Honey; let your love of the beautiful in Nature permeate the Barcarolle, but don't become too boisterous in the dance; remember always that program music is at its best when most in accord with those sentiments uttered by the great Beethoven in regard to his own "Pastoral Symphony" when he said, — "more an expression than a painting."

R. Nathaniel Dett

PRELUDE
Night

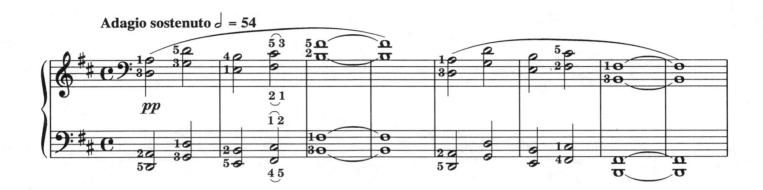

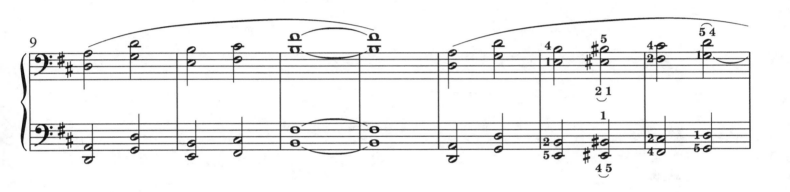

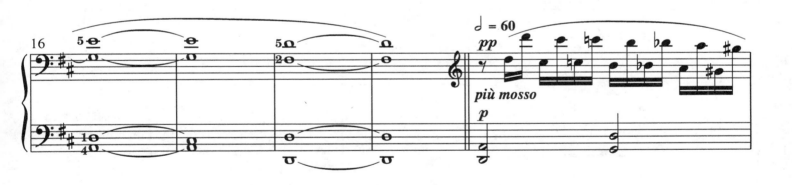

44

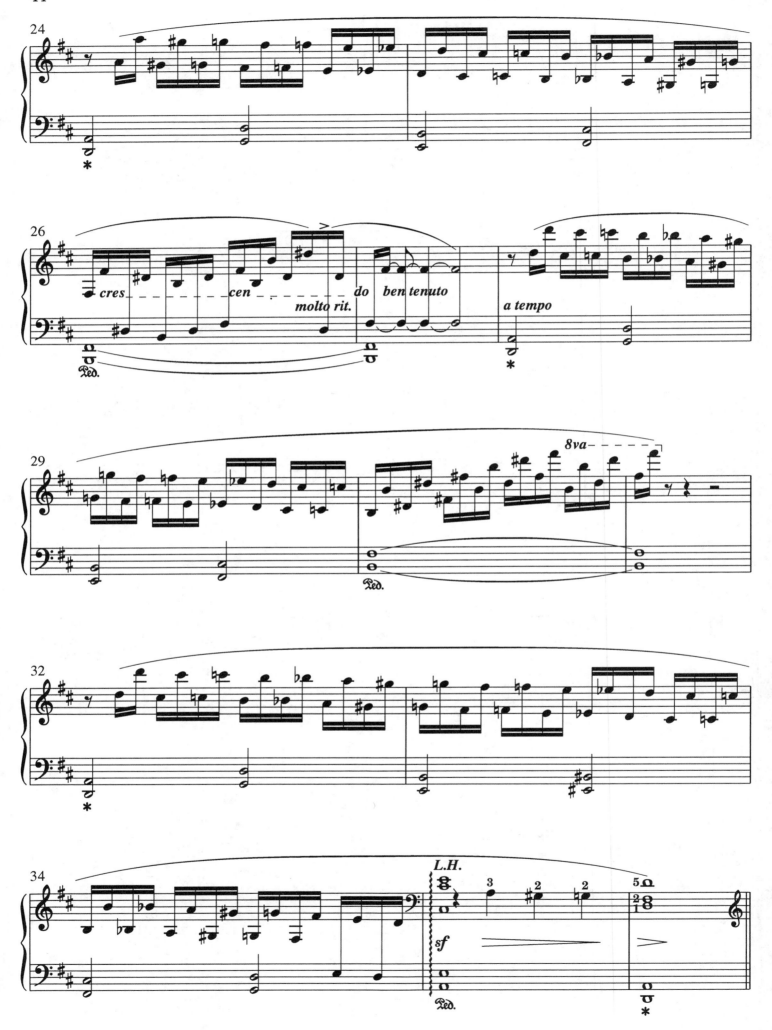

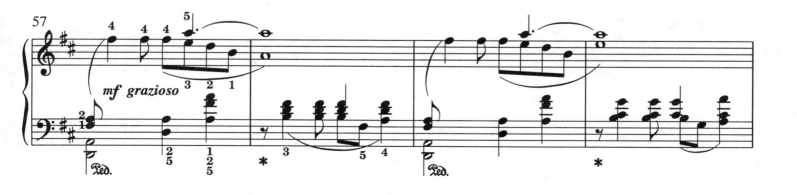

HIS SONG

Andante non troppo, ma più patetico ♩ = 120

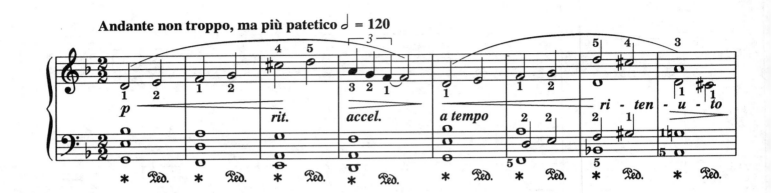

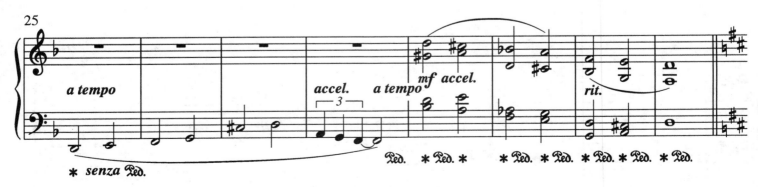

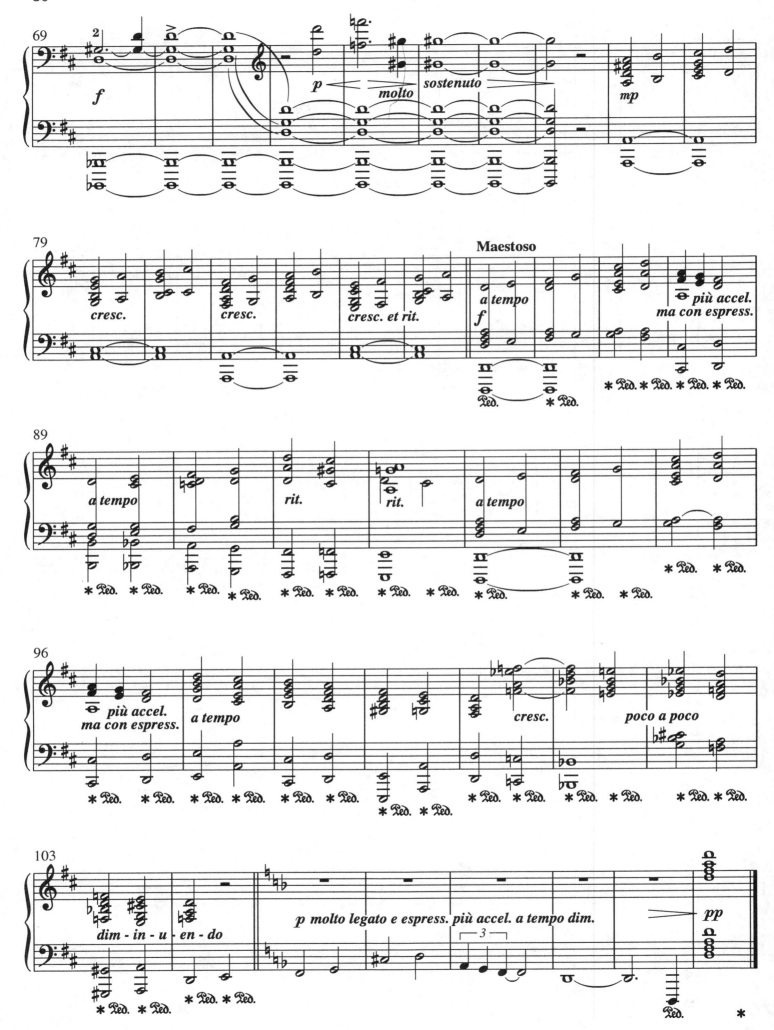

"Literally "Honey" is a colloquialism -
the familiar term of endearment
(South). It may mean much, little,
everything, or nothing;
the intimation here, is one
of coquetry".

R. Nathaniel Dett

HONEY
Humoresque

BARCAROLLE
Morning

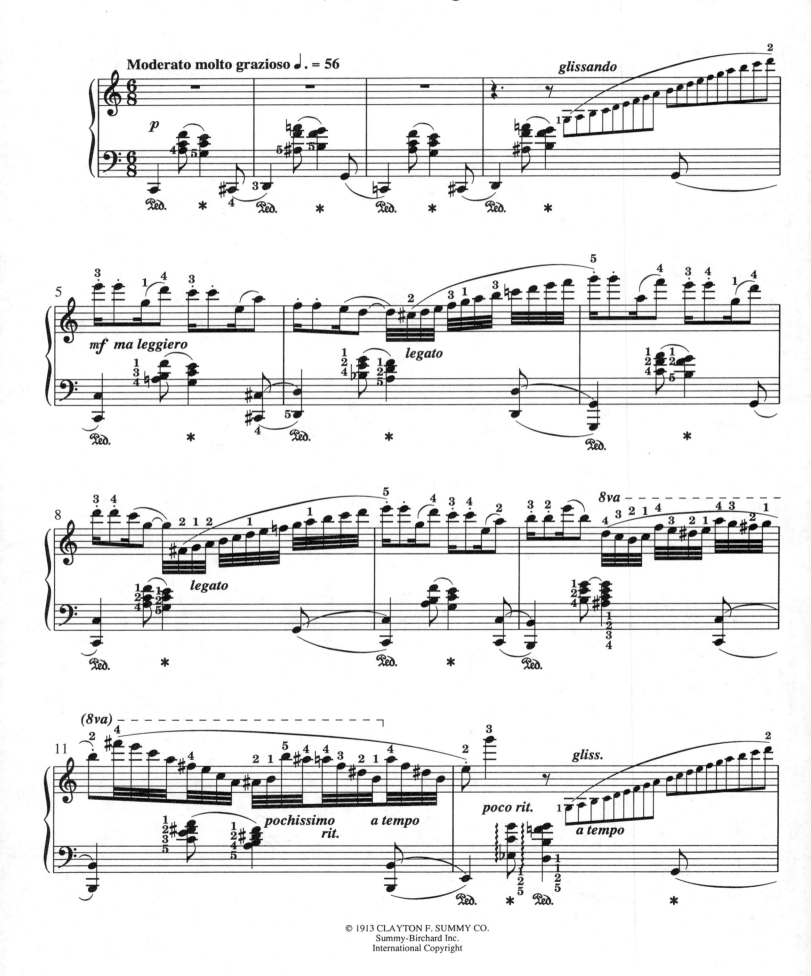

"A word of warning cannot be suppressed in regard to the tempo of the 'Dance.' Do not take it <u>too fast!</u> Much of the dancing in the bottoms is done with a grace and finish that a <u>Presto</u> tempo never could suggest."

R. Nathaniel Dett

DANCE
Juba

66

To PERCY GRAINGER
In Appreciation

R. Nathaniel Dett

ENCHANTMENT

A ROMANTIC SUITE FOR THE

PIANO

ON AN ORIGINAL PROGRAM

I	Incantation	50c Net
II	Song Of The Shrine	50c Net
III	Dance Of Desire	75c Net
IV	Beyond The Dream	50c Net

(Prices apply to U.S.A.)

THE JOHN CHURCH COMPANY
CINCINNATI   NEW YORK   LONDON
"The House devoted to the Progress of American Music"

Enchantment Suite

The Program

"What seek you? Say! And what do you expect?"
"I know not what: the Unknown I would have!
What's known to me is endless; I would go
Beyond the end. The last word still is wanting."

I. INCANTATION

A soul obsessed by a desire for the unattainable, journeying on an endless quest, wanders into a pagan temple, and there yields to an overpowering impulse of the moment to utter an Incantation before the shrine of an unknown goddess.

II. SONG OF THE SHRINE

From somewhere far within the shrine a mysterious voice answers — a

"voice of molten melody
Singing love that may not be."

III. DANCE OF DESIRE

A drum beats, and a gong sounds; strange shapes assemble for a carnival of passion, into whose company and revelry the soul finds itself drawn irresistibly. In the urge of the music the Incantation mingles with the now mocking Song of the Shrine.

After a mad swirl, there is a final crash, at the sound of which the apparitions vanish.

IV. BEYOND THE DREAM

And, as in a vision, the soul sees itself transfigured, appearing unto itself as an ever-shifting shoal of pale, opalescent fire, from which there rises in a visible exhalation, like smoke from smoldering incense, the still unsatisfied longing for the unattainable.

INCANTATION
I

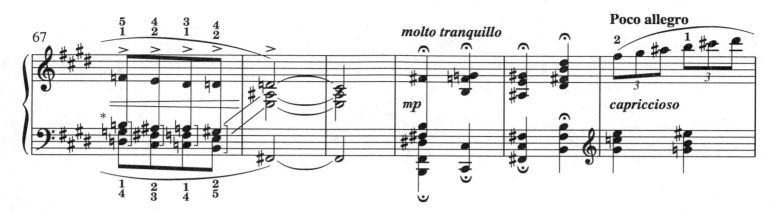

* Use left hand if preferable.

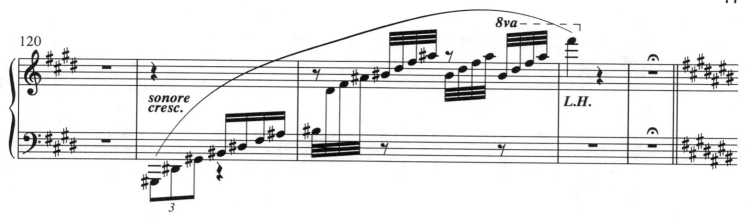

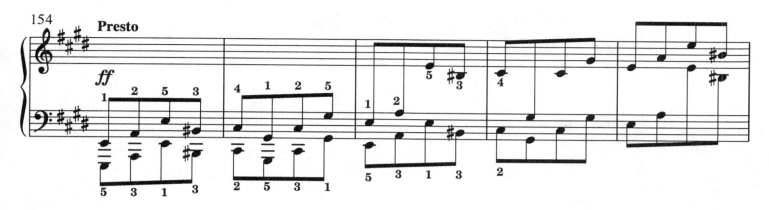

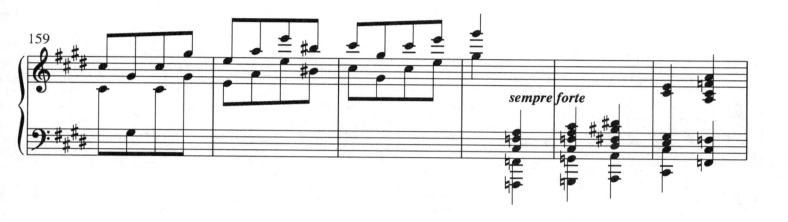

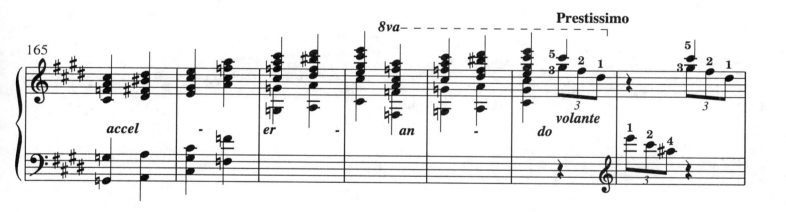

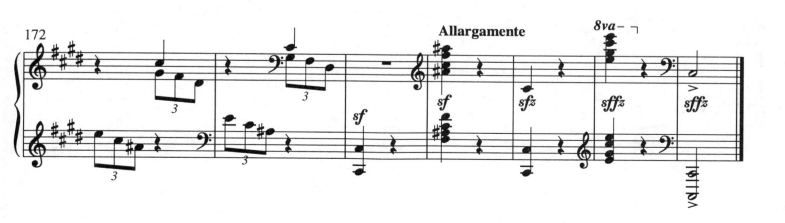

SONG OF THE SHRINE
II

Lento con molto espressione

DANCE OF DESIRE
III

* Use right hand if necessary

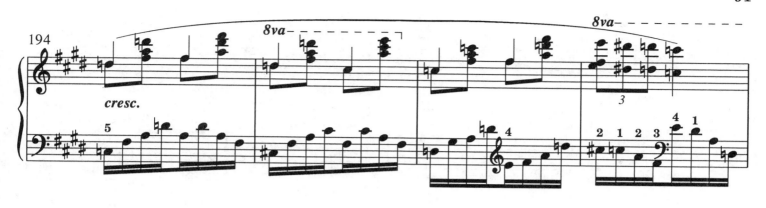

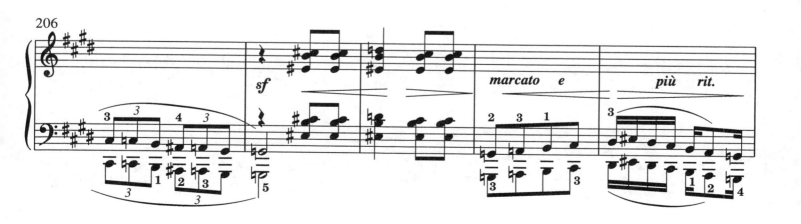

BEYOND THE DREAM
IV

Cinnamon Grove

A Suite for the Piano

BY

R. Nathaniel Dett

Price $1.25

The John Church Company

"The House Devoted to the Progress of American Music"

Cincinnati   New York   London

I

Moderato molto grazioso

on lines from "The Dream"
by JOHN DONNE

II

Adagio cantabile

on lines from *Gitanjali*
by RABINDRANATH TAGORE

III

Ritmo moderato e con sentimento
Quasi Gavotte

on lines from "Epimetheus"
by HENRY WADSWORTH LONGFELLOW

IV

Allegretto

on lines from a song
in *Religious Folk Songs of the Negro*

CINNAMON GROVE
A Suite For The Piano
I

"Dear love, for nothing less than thee
Would I have broke this happy dream:"

II

"When thou commandest me to sing
it seems that my heart would break
with pride; and I look to thy face,
and tears come to my eyes."

III

"Have I dreamed? or was it real,
What I saw as in a vision.
When to marches hymeneal
In the land of the Ideal
Moved my thought o'er Fields Elysian?"

IV

"Oh, the winter'll soon be over, children,
Yes, my Lord."

TROPIC WINTER

SUITE FOR PIANO

R. NATHANIEL DETT

$1.50

CLAYTON F. SUMMY CO.   CHICAGO · NEW YORK

THE DAYBREAK CHARIOTEER

Pomposo marziale moderato

a) Play all the single notes of the right hand scale passages with the third (middle) finger, braced against the thumb. -R. N. D.

A BAYOU GARDEN

POMPONS AND FANS
(Mazurka)

Grazioso M. M. ♩ = 96

*From here to * both hands 8va ad lib. – R. N. D.

136

LEGEND OF THE ATOLL

TO A CLOSED CASEMENT

"I am proud of this suite, as I think it represents an advance in musical thought..."

R. Nathaniel Dett

NOON SIESTA

PARADE OF THE JASMINE BANNERS

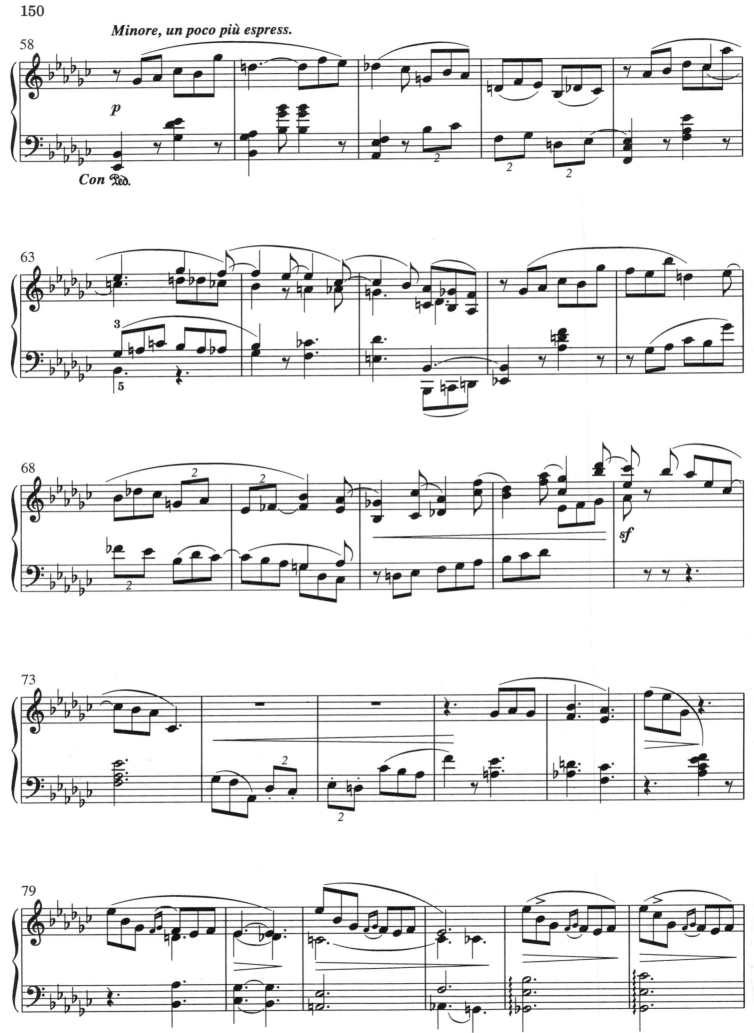

"BIBLE VIGNETTES"

EIGHT BIBLE VIGNETTES
for the PIANO

BY

R. NATHANIEL DETT

MILLS MUSIC
INC
Music Publishers
1619 Broadway—New York, N.Y.

"BIBLE VIGNETTES"

No. 1

Father Abraham

PIANO SOLO

BY

R. NATHANIEL DETT

MILLS MUSIC
INC
Music Publishers
1619 Broadway—New York, N.Y.

FATHER ABRABAM
I

DESERT INTERLUDE
II

Legend:

And Abraham rose up early in the morning, and took bread and a bottle of water, and

gave it unto Hagar, putting it on her shoulder and the child, and sent her away. And

she departed, and wandered in the wilderness of Beer-sheba.

— Genesis xxi, -14

DESERT INTERLUDE therefore, deals with that short period of time, wherein the banished Hagar, clasping the hand of Ishmael, her son, stood wonderingly, and despairingly in the desert, lost in dark contemplation.

The loaf of bread was almost gone, and the water "was spend in the bottle." The heat of the wilderness, each moment grew more oppressive. — What nostalgic thoughts of the home from which she lately had been thrust, — what fears for the immediate future—what maternal dread for the fate of her child, filled her breast!

What should she do? Was there no hope? Had God, even as Abraham, forsaken her?

DESERT INTERLUDE
2

AS HIS OWN SOUL
III

Legend:

And it came to pass .... that the
soul of Jonathan was knit with the soul of David, and
Jonathan loved him as his own soul.

— Samuel xviii, -1

To the memory of Carl

AS HIS OWN SOUL

3

Moderato semplice quasi volkslied ♩ = 84

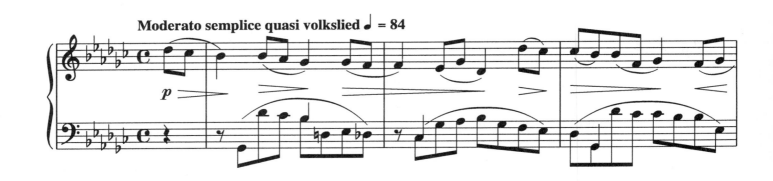

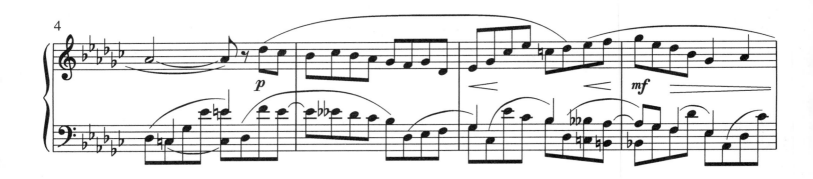

BARCAROLLE OF TEARS

4

I Am The True Vine

BY

R. NATHANIEL DETT

I AM THE TRUE VINE

5

Con moto, ma espressivo ♩ = 138

Martha Complained

MARTHA COMPLAINED
6

Other Sheep

FOR THE PIANO
BY
R. NATHANIEL DETT

OTHER SHEEP
7

Maggiore

MADRIGAL DIVINE
8

Moderato, molto tranquillo

S0-AGK-173

FUN SCIENCE

THAT TEACHES GOD'S WORD

BY Mary Grace Becker
and
Susan Martins Miller

NexGen® is an imprint of
Cook Communications Ministries, Colorado Springs, CO 80918
Cook Communications, Paris, Ontario
Kingsway Communications, Eastbourne, England

FUN SCIENCE THAT TEACHES GOD'S WORD
Copyright © 2004 Cook Communications Ministries

Cover Design: Granite Design
Interior Design: idesign Etc.

Printed in the United States of America
First Printing, 2004

4 5 6 7 8 9 10 11 Printing/Year 11 10 09 08 07 06

ISBN-10: 0-7814-4081-5
ISBN-13: 978-0-7814-4081-3

TABLE
of Contents

Not What It Seems

Tag-alongs

INTRODUCTION

Slime. Balloons. Goo. Cooking Oil. Water. Really fun stuff for kids—really great teaching tools for you to lead them along the path of discipleship!

The more we understand of science, the more we stand in awe of God. Nothing attests to the endless imagination of God like the world he created. Every square foot of the natural world is filled with wonders just waiting to be explored. And the things you and your kids can cook up with just a few supplies will bring new understanding of important spiritual truths right along with the "oohs" and "ahs."

We've designed these little scientific wonders to work in your elementary classroom (although we'll confess many middle schoolers have been fascinated by these activities). Your kids get to be the scientists, often working in pairs or groups. There are no plans for noxious gases or wall-shuddering explosions, but we do recommend a sturdy vinyl tablecloth. After all, you can't make slime without getting a little slimy!

You'll find a clear goal for each activity in the "Truth Explosion." The "Formula for Success" lists the supplies you'll need—most of it readily available from your grocery or pharmacy. Think how much fun you'll have watching your sometimes distracted kids totally engrossed with their experiments and absorbing spiritual truth. Then check the "Lab Results" for a brief wrap-up discussion. Every activity has a Bible verse and suggestions for stories you can use it with.

Some activities provide scientific treasures for your kids to take with them. Others can be repeated with family and friends with the kids in the teaching role, flaunting their scientific prowess and making the application to how we live as followers of Christ.

The laboratory is yours!

EARTH, WIND, FIRE AND GOO!

Goop. Ooze. Slime. Kids love it all. These Earth, Wind, Fire and Goo science experiments use ordinary supplies to explore the wonders of the world God made and teach faith lessons along the way.

SIMPLE SCIENCE KNOW-HOW'S

What can you do with things like kitchen supplies and ordinary office items? **Plenty.** These Simple Science Know How activities use easy-to-find supplies and keep mess to a minimum. Amaze your kids with the simplicity of trusting God's way.

NOT WHAT IT SEEMS

Do your kids think they've got it all figured out? These Not What It Seems science activities will help them see that God can act in unexpected ways when they look with the eyes of faith.

TAG-ALONGS

Are you looking for a great science reminder to send home with your kids? **Get ready** to punch up the photocopier. These Tag-alongs science activities ensure they'll have something to take with them and share with their families.

A CHANCE OF CLOUDS

How is fog made?

How are clouds made?

As kids make a cloud in a jar, they'll see God's power and remember that he is worthy of worship.

Truth Explosion: God wants everyone to worship him. I can tell others about Jesus.

GODPRINT:

Worship

TIME:

10 minutes

GROUP SIZE:

Groups of 4

MESS METER

1 **2** 3

As you begin this activity, or a little ahead of time, fill the metal dishes with ice cubes. Kids will need to see this up close, so plan on a dish and jar for about every four kids. Let the ice cubes chill the dish thoroughly.

Before Jesus went to heaven, he told his followers to tell other people the good news that they can be part of God's kingdom. Then Jesus rose into a cloud. Let's make a cloud in a jar to remind us that as Jesus went to heaven, he gave all his followers a job to do.

FORMULA for success

- hot water
- metal dishes
- clear jars
- ice cubes
- small action figures

Set an action figure behind each glass. Have the kids look through the clear glass to see the action figure on the other side. Point out how clearly they can see. Then add one inch of hot tap water in the jar.

When the metal dish is cold, remove the ice from the dish. Immediately place the metal dish over the top of the jar, cold side down. As the hot water evaporates, it will come in contact with the cold dish. The moisture will condense and form a cloud. **Scientifically speaking, we'll see warm water evaporate into the air where it will be met by cold air, causing condensation. Mini-clouds!** Ask kids to look through the glass again. This time the cloud will obscure their vision of the action figure. Let kids repeat the experiment as time allows.

Cloud

Another way to do this activity is to tape black paper on the back of a jar and pour in some warm water. Hold a lit match in the jar for a few seconds and then drop it in. Quickly cover the jar opening with an ice pack. Water droplets will cling to the trail of man-made smoke for a mini-cloud formation.

Lab Results

• What job was Jesus preparing the disciples for? _(To tell others about him.)_

• What did the disciples see the last time they were together with Jesus? _(The ascension. Jesus was hidden by a cloud.)_

• When has watching the clouds made you feel amazed at God's power?

• How can we carry on the same job that the disciples were doing?

God wants the whole world to know him and worship him. That's why Jesus sent the disciples to the ends of the earth to spread the Good News. And now it's our turn. Let's make Jesus' message crystal clear to those we meet.

You are worthy, our Lord and God, to receive glory and honor and power.

Revelation 4:11

USE THIS SCIENCE ACTIVITY WITH:

• Jesus ascends to heaven. Acts 1:1–11 _(A cloud hid Jesus from the disciples' sight.)_

• Transfiguration. Matthew 17:1–8 _(A bright cloud enveloped Jesus, Moses and Elijah.)_

YE OLD WIZER GEYSER

Old Faithfal
What is a geyser?

Use this activity to remind kids that God is a geyser of faithfulness—he always provides and never lets us down. Our loving response should be up to the task!

Truth Explosion: God is faithful to us. We need to be faithful to him.

GODPRINT:
Faithfulness

TIME:
15–20 minutes

GROUP SIZE:
Small groups

MESS METER
1 2 **3**

Spread the tablecloth on your worktable as you speak to your group. **Who has heard of the hot water geyser called Old Faithful?** Pause for responses. **Good job! Old Faithful is a geyser found in Yellowstone National Park. A geyser is an underground spring that spurts a tall tower of heat and hot water every few hours. This particular geyser is named Old Faithful because it is faithful, always spurting on schedule. Park rangers (and visitors!) can depend on the geyser to spray and amaze.**

FORMULA for success
- small glass jar with screw-on lid
- medium nail (3.5 mm)
- hammer
- drinking straw
- modeling clay
- straight pin
- bowl
- hot and cold water
- tablecloth

Today let's make a geyser to help us remember that God wants us to be as faithful as that famous geyser in living the way he taught us.

Depending on the size of your class, you may wish to have several groups make separate geysers.

Fill the jar with cold water three-quarters full. Use the hammer and nail to poke a hole in the jar lid. Push a straw through the hole and screw the lid on the jar. Make sure the bottom of the straw is in the water. Press modeling clay around the straw where it meets the lid to seal off the opening. With another piece of clay, plug up the top of the straw. Use a pin to make a hole through the clay plug.

This is where the water should come out. Let's see. Everybody ready?
Set the jar in a bowl of hot water and stand back. Expect a shower!

Lab Results

• How can a geyser help us understand what it means to be faithful?

• Tell me some other words for "faithful."

• Why is it important for us to be faithful to God in the way that we live and the choices we make?

God is faithful to us. He wants us to be faithful to him by making choices that show others what God is like.

And whatever you do, whether in word or
deed, do it all in the name of the Lord Jesus,
giving thanks to God the Father through him.

Colossians 3:17

SUPER Science facts

As the water warms in the jar, the air molecules inside move faster and further apart. This "excited" state of expansion causes the water to move and burst from the straw.

USE THIS SCIENCE ACTIVITY WITH:

• Noah obeys God. Genesis 6:9–8:22 (*Noah was faithful to God's specific instructions for a long time.*)

• Kings from the east worship Jesus. Matthew 1:18–2:12 (*The kings faithfully followed the star, and faithfully followed God's instructions to return home another way.*)

• Caleb and Joshua are faithful spies. Numbers 13:1, 2,17–30; 14:6–9 (*Caleb and Joshua were confident in God's provision even when the other spies were not.*)

CHALK IT UP TO OBEDIENCE

A few simple supplies help your kids learn that God's way is the best way.

Truth Explosion: We can obey God even when it's hard.

GODPRINT:
Submissiveness

TIME:
10 minutes

GROUP SIZE:
Individual

MESS METER

1 2 3

Cut a long sheet of waxed paper and lay it on a table. Place the chalk and a bowl of lemon juice nearby. Ask kids to gather around.

There is an age-old expression that people use to describe hard times. When "life hands you a lemon" it means hard times have come to call. Distribute the cotton swabs. Have kids dip the swabs in the lemon juice, then dab the swabs to their tongues.

• How does the lemon juice taste? How does this remind you of hard times?

Have kids throw away their swabs. **Now let's pick up the chalk and print the words, "We can obey God even when its hard" on our waxed paper. Everyone will take a word. Evie, you have the first word, John, the next**...(and so on). Have kids give it a try. The chalk will not adhere very well to the paper. The waxed paper might even tear. **Having a hard time? When we obey God even when it's hard, we have him on our side to see us through the torn and tough times. Let's start over.**

Turn over the waxed paper or tear a clean sheet. **Now dip your chalk tip into the lemon juice and print your word on the paper.** The acid in the lemon juice reacts with the alkaline limestone in the chalk, softening it so more chalk prints on the paper. **Way to go, Joe. Jesus makes a way when we obey!**

Lab Results

• What is your reaction when things don't go your way? Do things end up better or worse when you react that way?

• Name two things that can help you stick with God in times like that. *(Take a breath and ask Jesus for help.)*

• How does Jesus' example in the Bible help every time?

Knock. Knock. Who's there? Hard times. Hard times who? Hard times are the best times to rely on God. Let's put ourselves under God's authority and do his will.

I can do everything through him who gives me strength.

Philippians 4:13

USE THIS SCIENCE ACTIVITY WITH:

• Jesus prays in the garden. John 17:1–18:11 *(Jesus submitted to God's will even though he knew it meant pain and death.)*

• Ten Commandments (relating to God). Exodus 19:1–8; 20:1–11 *(God tells us how he wants us to relate to him and gives rules that will help us submit.)*

• Jonah learns to obey. Jonah 1:1–3:10 *(Jonah tried his own way and learned that doing things God's way is best.)*

WET ROCKS

How many marbles can you put on a wet tissue?

It's not rock-et science! Let Jesus encourage your kids' faith and give them the confidence to believe that he is the Son of God.

Truth Explosion: Because Jesus helps me with my doubts, I can believe in him.

Do friends joke or brag that they can do amazing, super-human things that no one else can do? Like x-ray vision or mind control? Is your response a firm, "Yeah, right!" Let's do an experiment to see, firsthand, the heavy weight that doubt puts on our spiritual lives.

GODPRINT:
Confidence

TIME:
15 minutes

GROUP SIZE:
Individual or pairs

MESS METER
1 **2** 3

FORMULA *for success*
- plastic cups
- a cup of water
- tissues
- rubber bands
- small stones or marbles

Place the empty cups on the table and the cup of water nearby. Have one of your students lay a tissue over the empty cup and gently secure it with a rubber band. Ask another student to dip his or her fingers into the glass of water and drop four

or five water droplets onto the tissue. Then have the class gather.

Doubts can lead us away from Jesus. Allow kids to express when doubt has taken them away from Jesus' wisdom and promise for their lives. With each response have students lightly place one stone at a time on the wet tissue. Be listening for confusion between questions and doubts. It's healthy to ask questions so we can have stronger faith.

The big question is this: how long before the faithful tissue breaks under the weight of doubt? Depending on the strength of the tissue, it will hold 7 to 12 small stones before splitting. Two layered tissues will hold twice as many stones—or more.

Even Jesus' friends and followers struggled with doubt. When Jesus appeared to the disciples after his resurrection, Thomas wanted proof it was really him. Like the disciples we have a choice. We can put our faith and hope in Jesus, or we can stand still and break under the pressure of doubt. Make your choice a confident first step toward Jesus!

Lab Results
• What kinds of pressures and pains cause people to doubt their faith in Jesus?
• In an ordinary day, when does doubt weigh heavy on your mind?
• When is it easiest to believe that Jesus is really with you? Why?

Jesus celebrated people who would put their faith in him long after his death. He made it a point to call these believers blessed! (John 20:29) **Because Jesus helps us with doubts, we can believe in him.**

Find rest, O my soul, in God alone;
my hope comes from him.

Psalm 62:5

USE THIS SCIENCE ACTIVITY WITH:

• Jesus rises from the dead and appears to Thomas. John 19:1–18; 20:1–8, 19–31 *(Thomas doubted Jesus' ressurection. Jesus says that those who believe without seeing are blessed.)*

• A young Jesus at the temple. Luke 2:41–52 *(Jesus was confident and doubt-free about his purpose in life. He knew his own identity.)*

• Paul and the Philippian jailer. Acts 16:16–40 *(Paul was confident that God was in control, even though he was in prison. He helped the jailer be confident of the true God.)*

MY BEAUTIFUL BALLOON

Up, up and away! Use this experiment to see how an invisible faith in God grows and grows.

Truth Explosion: God wants us to make choices that reflect our relationship with him.

GODPRINT:
Faith

TIME:
5–10 minutes

GROUP SIZE:
Individual or pairs

MESS METER
1 **2** 3

For a quick warm-up to this activity, start with a simple experiment on static electricity. Open the packet of tabletop confetti and pour a little of it into a clean and dry soda bottle. Now stretch your balloon and place it over the mouth of the bottle. Turn the bottle over and shake the confetti into the balloon. Blow up the balloon, knot, and rub it against a student's hair. Static electricity will cause the confetti to jump and stick to the sides of the balloon! *(Fun Science Fact: If two objects attract and stick together, they have opposite charges.)* **Let's do another experiment that will help us remember that God is everywhere—even if we can't see him. Allow God's supernatural powers to help invisible faith grow in you!**

Fill the bottle with 1/4 cup of water.

• How do worries and fears keep us from growing in faith? Does Jesus understand this about day-to-day worries?

Sprinkle 1 tsp. of baking soda into the bottle and stir with the straw. Pour in the lemon juice. Quickly stretch an uninflated balloon and place it over the mouth of the bottle.

We don't "see" anything inside the bottle, do we? But we have faith that there's something in there. Let's prove it!

Watch as the balloon inflates—and the confetti twinkles and shines when held close to a light source!

Lab Results

• We can't see the gas, but we know that it's in there. How does this remind you of many of Jesus' miracles?
• What "earthly" things crowd out God and leave little room for his power to work miracles in our lives?
• Can you think of something you might have to give up to allow faith to grow in you?

Our experiment is a fun way to remember that although we don't see faith, we can trust its power to connect to God.

Now faith is being sure of what we hope for and certain of what we do not see.

Hebrews 11:1

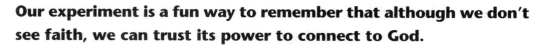

SUPER Science facts

When a base (baking soda) and an acid (lemon juice) come together the resulting reaction forms a clear, colorless gas known as carbon dioxide. As the gas rises it fills the empty balloon.

HAVE WATER, WILL TRAVEL

Watch out for blue skies and sunny dispositions as your kids discover that no matter what the future brings, God will be there to help.

Truth Explosion: Because God has helped me in the past, I can be sure he will help me in the future.

GODPRINT:
Diligence

TIME:
20 minutes

GROUP SIZE:
Large group or small group

MESS METER

1 2 3

If you have a large class, you may want to set up several areas for smaller groups to work.

When you serve the Lord, anything is possible—even when things seem impossible to you. God is available to help yesterday, today and all our tomorrows. When the water rises and trouble appears ready to wash us over, let's choose to serve the Lord and wait for his goodness and mercy.

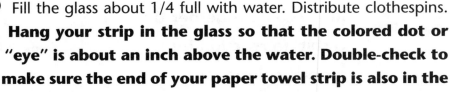

FORMULA
for success
• paper towels
• scissors
• green felt-tipped pens
• glasses
• water
• clothespins

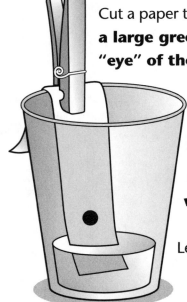

Cut a paper towel into 2-inch strips. **On your strip of paper towel color in a large green dot about 2 inches from the bottom. This will be the "eye" of the storm that appears on our troubled horizon.**

Fill the glass about 1/4 full with water. Distribute clothespins. **Hang your strip in the glass so that the colored dot or "eye" is about an inch above the water. Double-check to make sure the end of your paper towel strip is also in the water.** Secure strips with the clothespins.

Let the experiment stand for 15 minutes.

Return to find that the water will have traveled into the thousands of tiny space pockets between the paper towel fibers and advanced upward. Surprisingly, the spot is gone from the paper towel! In its place the paper has turned blue and above that a bright yellow.

Lab Results
• When is it difficult for you to choose to serve God?
• In what ways do you want God to help you this week?

While we are busy worrying and wringing our hands, God is at work in our lives. The eye of the storm is gone and on the horizon appears only blue skies and plenty of sunshine!

Although not every problem ends with sunny skies, when we serve God we have the help we need when the clouds build. Remember to serve God with a faithful heart no matter what the weather.

Then choose for yourselves this day whom you will serve...as for me and my household, we will serve the LORD.

Joshua 24:15

SUPER Science facts

As water is drawn upward into the paper, so is the green ink. If time permits, try this experiment with other colors. Colors made up of one color pigment will travel much faster than those colors with two or more.

USE THIS SCIENCE ACTIVITY WITH:

• Joshua crosses the Jordan and builds an altar. Joshua 3:1–4:24. *(Joshua was diligent in leading God's people in a tough time.)*

• Josiah cleans the temple. 2 Kings 22:1–13; 23:1–6; 23:21–23 *(Diligent Josiah brought the people back to God's Word.)*

• Noah. Genesis 6:1–9:17 *(Noah didn't give up on a job that seemed ridiculous to others. He remained diligent and followed God's instructions.)*

A FUNNEL OF FUN!

With a huff and a puff, kids find out that they need God's strength to make choices that please him.

Truth Explosion: God's Spirit helps us make choices that show his presence in our lives.

GODPRINT:
Integrity

TIME:
5 minutes

GROUP SIZE:
Individual or pairs

MESS METER
1 2 3

With his help, God wants us to produce the fruit of the Spirit. Unfortunately, experience teaches us that our human nature prefers its own sinful way.

FORMULA
for success
• clean household funnels
• table tennis balls

• Did you feel really selfish this week?
• Did you feel like quitting something hard?

We can agree that on our own it's an impossible task to attain the joy, love and faithfulness God wants us to have. Still we try and try to go it alone!

Hold out the funnel and the table tennis ball. **What would you think if I told you I'm known far and wide for having a pair of mighty lungs? I can take a really deep breath and blow harder than anyone you know. Suppose I said I could blow this little ball up to the ceiling?**

Drop the ball into the funnel. Tilt your head back and put the funnel's narrow end near your lips. **How long will it be before I blow the ball inside this funnel up to the ceiling?**

Have your kids shout out guesses. Then blow! The harder you blow the higher the ball will go—but it will not hit the ceiling. The ball will simply remain suspended in the air a short distance away from the funnel. **I'm trying! I'm trying!** Take a deep breath and try again.

Helpful hint: The only way to get the ball out of the funnel is to blow across the top of the funnel! If you have extra funnels and balls, give kids a chance to try.

I admit it. I can't do it! I hope we've all learned that we can't overcome our own selfish ways using just our strength.

Lab Results

• Can anyone tell about a time when God helped you conquer a selfish, mean or discouraging feeling?
• Why is trying on your own to be joyful or patient not enough to make it happen?
• Tell about a time when God's Spirit helped you be loving, joyful or patient.

Our actions and behaviors alone do not allow us to live the kind of joyful, unselfish life God has planned for us, try and try as we might. Only with the Holy Spirit can we demonstrate the behavior and attitude needed to produce his fruit.

The fruit of the Spirit is love, joy, peace, patience, kindness, goodness, faithfulness, gentleness and self-control.

Galatians 5:22, 23

SUPER Science facts

Bernoulli's Principle states that the rapid moving air in a funnel results in a decrease in air pressure. This causes the ball to be pushed into the funnel by the higher air pressure sitting on top. Fun fact: A funnel attached to a constant blowing air supply can be held upside down and the ball will not fly out!

USE THIS SCIENCE ACTIVITY WITH:

• Fruit of the Spirit. Galatians 5:22–25 *(If we have the fruit of the Spirit in our lives, then we are the same on the outside as we are on the inside.)*

• Beatitudes. Matthew 5:1–12 *(Jesus focused on the inner qualities that come from God.)*

MAGNETIC PERSONALITY

Join together to honor God's call to respect others.

Truth Explosion: Because God is a God of peace, I can take the first step to end an argument

GODPRINT:
Respectfulness

TIME:
15-20 minutes

GROUP SIZE:
Pairs

MESS METER
1 2 3

USE THIS SCIENCE ACTIVITY WITH:

• Abraham chooses peace with Lot. Genesis 12:1–9; 13:1–18. *(Abraham treated Lot with respect and gave him the first choice of the land.)*

• The parable of the place of honor. Luke 14:1–14 *(Jesus reminds us to treat others with respect rather than pleasing ourselves.)*

• David spares Saul. 1 Samuel 26:1–25 *(David showed respect for Saul's role as God's chosen king, even though Saul treated him terribly.)*

What do you notice about magnets? *(Like ends will push away from each other.)* **Try to join the positive ends of your magnets.** *(They will repel.)* **Now join the positive and negative ends of the magnets.** Magnets will "stick" together.

God reminds us to treat each other with respect even when wills repel and emotions take a positive charge!

FORMULA
for success
• magnets
• index cards
• Optional: poster board, bowl of water, paper clip

Have kids write on an index card one sentence about an argument that kept them apart from someone they cared about. Trade with a partner. Place the index cards in the middle of two magnets and lift them off the table. Try to pass the cards in a circle using only the magnets. Return the cards to the table and with the magnets underneath the tabletop drag the cards mysteriously back and forth without touching them. Or use poster board for the same effect. Another fun option is to drop a paper clip into a bowl of water. Use the magnet to draw the paper clip out of the bowl.

Lab Results

• Two teams show up on the same practice field. What problems can you see popping up? How far apart do you see the sides?

Remind the people...to be peaceable and considerate, and to show true humility toward all men.

Titus 3:1, 2

LAVA GLOW

Encourage your kids to let God's love light shine.

Truth Explosion: Because Jesus teaches us how to love, we can love others.

Set out the materials on a covered table. Ask kids to take a cup each. **When we ask Jesus in our hearts as Savior, his love light is then free to bubble up and shine. Let's do a simple experiment to see how that might happen.** Have kids take turns pouring 1/2-inch of vegetable oil into their cups.

Walk your cup over to a window or hold it up to the light. The oil catches the light and makes it glisten.

Have kids carefully pour a 1/4-inch layer of salt on top of the oil. **Sometimes we feel selfish, or we wish to get even with people who've wronged us. When all these selfish feelings come to the top, they dim God's love light in our lives. Carefully pour water down the inside of your cup so you don't disturb the layer of salt. Keep filling your cup with water until it's almost full.** Observe bubbles of "bright" oil break through the salt crust and rise to the surface. **Jesus changes hearts that are self-serving to ones that shine in a sin-heavy world.**

Lab Results
- How is the salt like the selfishness we see in the world today?
- Tell an example of a time when God's love broke through your selfishness.

Let your light shine before men, that they may see your good deeds and praise your Father in heaven.

Matthew 5:16

FORMULA for success

- clear plastic drinking cups
- vegetable oil
- salt
- pitcher of water
- tablecloth

GODPRINT:
Love

TIME:
15 minutes

GROUP SIZE:
Individual or pairs

MESS METER
1 **2** 3

USE THIS SCIENCE ACTIVITY WITH:

- Sermon on the Mount. Matthew 5:13–16. *(Jesus talks about letting inner qualities shine through.)*

- The gift of love. 1 Corinthians 13 *(Paul teaches about the supremacy of sincere love.)*

- Parable of the Prodigal Son. Luke 15:11–32. *(Jesus gives us a picture of God's forgiving love.)*

- Parable of the Good Samaritan. Luke 10:25–37 *(Jesus tells a story to encourage us to make love practical.)*

- Ruth shows her love for Naomi. Ruth 1:1–4:12 *(Love for Naomi motivated Ruth to leave her own country.)*

NEEDLE THE WATER

My way or God's way? Needle your kids into going in the right direction.

Truth Explosion: Because God's timing is always right, I can depend on him to show me what to do.

GODPRINT:
Purposefulness

TIME:
20 minutes

GROUP SIZE:
Individual or pairs

MESS METER
1 **2** 3

Before class, cut 1-inch circles from the waxed paper. Set the empty glass in front of you. **If we try to meet our needs on our own** (place a few drops of water in the glass) **we feel empty. Only when we depend on God are we filled spiritually and pointed in the right direction.**

Fill the glass to the top. When the water has settled, set the sewing needle on a small piece of tissue paper. Float it on the water. In a short time the paper will saturate and sink to the bottom of the glass. The needle, however, will continue to float on the surface. **God sustains us with his mighty hand and will not let you fall. Enemies or worries or even death cannot separate us from his love.**

Remove the needle from the glass. **Have you ever been lost on a hike or camping trip? If you had a compass, it would have helped guide you and your group in the right direction. We can depend on God's timing and direction whether lost or found.**

Magnetize needles by having each child use the magnet to rub his or her needle 20 or 30 times in the same direction across the magnet. Helpful hint: It is important to use the same end of the magnet to rub while lifting the magnet away with each stroke. If you wish, you can magnetize the needles ahead of time.

FORMULA
for success
- pitcher of water
- glass with saucer
  - tissue paper
  - waxed paper
- sewing needles
- small magnets

Before proceeding with the lesson, point out to your children which way north is in your classroom. **Now carefully thread your needle into your waxed paper like this.** Demonstrate for your students how to poke the needle in and out of a waxed paper circle. **Now float the waxed paper on the surface of the water in your glass. Gently use your finger to move it to the right. Let go. Watch what happens!** Needles will point north no matter how they are turned.

Lab Results

• Who at home helps meet your needs and guides you throughout the week?
• What kind of job would you like to have in 20 years and why is God's timing important?
• Have you ever felt "pulled" in God's direction?
• How is this needle like God's perfect timing?

The plans of the LORD stand firm forever.

Psalm 33:11

SUPER Science facts

A magnet allowed to turn freely will react to the Earth's magnetic field. Even a simple compass will line up and point to magnetic north.

USE THIS SCIENCE ACTIVITY WITH:

• Daniel and his friends stand up to the king. Daniel 1:1–21. *(Even though they were captives, these friends kept their focus on following God's direction.)*

• Jesus tells Peter, "Feed my sheep." John 21:1–19. *(Peter had made mistakes, but Jesus let him know God still had a purpose for him.)*

• Abigail helps David see God's way. 1 Samuel 25:1–35 *(David was about to lose his temper. Abigail showed him God's way.)*

SPARKLE ROCK GEOLOGY

Twinkle, twinkle little rock! Make a sparkling monument diorama that attests to God's faithfulness.

Truth Explosion: Because we live by faith, we can follow God's leading.

GODPRINT:
Faithfulness

TIME:
20 minutes

GROUP SIZE:
Pairs

MESS METER
1 **2** 3

Before class collect enough smooth and clean rocks for your group.

When people wish to remember something important, they often erect a monument or statue. A monument "marks the spot!" For example, think of a large rock which displays the following words: *George Washington Slept Here!* or *Here Lies the Greatest Home Run Hitter of All Time!* Heads turn as people stop to look and remember.

In the Old Testament, Joshua built a remembrance altar. This was a solid stone monument to remind the people of God's help in crossing the muddy Jordan River. It would serve as a reminder to all who came along of God's faithfulness in times past and the days to come. Let's build our own mini-monument as a way for others to remember God's faithfulness.

Think of how God has been faithful in your life. Ask kids to pick up a permanent marker and write one or two words on several rocks.

Then have kids pair up and mix batches of sparkly paint. Mix two tablespoons

FORMULA
for success
- rocks
- permanent markers
- liquid starch
- water
- green food coloring
- salt
- small containers for mixing
- small paintbrushes
- shoeboxes
- small greenery

of liquid starch, two tablespoons of water, a few drops of green food coloring and 1/2 cup of salt for each pair of students. Use paintbrushes to apply the paint to the rocks. **Once dry, this special paint will give your rocks an ancient, mossy look!**

After the rocks dry completely, have kids stack them in the shoebox to form a monument. Glue "trees" and "bushes" on either side. **Think of other ways you might enhance your memorial diorama when you get home. Share your thoughts with your neighbor.**

Lab Results

• How can you learn to stop and listen to God when times get busy?
• Name some ways that God has been faithful to you.
• Name some ways that you can be faithful to God.

God is always faithful. Make it your goal to please him.

The Lord is faithful, and he will strengthen and protect you from the evil one.

2 Thessalonians 3:3

SUPER
Science facts

Geology is the study of the history of the earth as recorded in rocks.

USE THIS SCIENCE ACTIVITY WITH:

• Joshua crosses the Jordan and builds an altar. Joshua 3:1–4:24 *(Joshua led God's people in making a monument that would remind them of his faithfulness for generations.)*

• Solomon builds the temple. 1 Kings 6:1–17; 8:62–66 *(Solomon built the temple so the people could be faithful in worshiping God.)*

• The Garden tomb (the Resurrection). Luke 23:32–46; 24:1–12 *(The empty tomb is a monument that reminds us of what God has done for us and inspires us to be faithful to him.)*

WATER MUSIC

Listen and do! With this fun activity your kids learn that we need to listen and do what God's Word says.

Truth Explosion: Because God is with me, I can do what he asks me to do.

GODPRINT:
Perseverance

TIME:
15 minutes

GROUP SIZE:
Large group

MESS METER
1 2 3

Are you good at listening *and doing?* It's not enough to know God's Word. We have to "put feet" on what we hear and go out and make it happen. Let's make some music using a simple glass harp. You'll get a turn to play what came before, then chime a note of your own. We'll keep adding notes until we have a wonderful melody. This will take some perseverance to get right so hang in there!

FORMULA for success

- 6–8 identical drinking glasses
- metal spoons
- pitcher of water
- Optional: pony bead, balloon

Fill glasses with varying amounts of water and experiment with different pitches as kids gently tap glasses with spoons. Have students add or empty water from glasses to come up with a pleasing tune.

If you wish, choose a Tune Captain to come up with a melody line. Then assign one glass to one or two students. Tell kids that when the Tune Captain taps a certain glass, the students assigned to that glass will perform a corresponding simple action or musical step, such as moving a foot or arm in a certain way. Let the kids make up the actions that will go with each glass. Practice makes permanent! Then have the Tune Captain play the tune slowly while the class displays their steps in sequence. Quicken the pace for added fun!

Lab Results

- There's more to music than just listening. Sometimes you need to move your feet and tap to the beat! Why does God want us to share his love with others instead of keeping it all to ourselves?

• How can you "do what the Word says" this week?
• When can you make a glass harp at home and play it with your family?

We can put God's Word into action when we rely on his strength. Whatever the circumstances, discouragement or opposition, play on! And spread the Word of God.

Do not merely listen to the word, and so deceive yourselves. Do what it says.

James 1:22

Something Extra!

For another fun and simple experiment on sound, push a pony bead inside a balloon. With the pony bead resting at the bottom of the balloon, blow up the balloon and knot. Shake the balloon in a circular motion to get the pony bead rolling. Place the balloon to your ear. Cool! Jesus talks to us in ways we don't expect.

USE THIS SCIENCE ACTIVITY WITH:

• Joseph commits to be part of God's plan. Matthew 1:18–2:15 *(Joseph persevered in a difficult situation and did what God asked him to do.)*

• Ezra and Nehemiah rebuild the wall. Ezra 7; Nehemiah 6–8 *(Ezra and Nehemiah persevered against people who tried to stop them.)*

• Joseph dreams and is sold into slavery. Genesis 37:1–36 *(Joseph persevered through slavery and imprisonment and discovered God's purpose.)*

SUPER Science facts

Hitting the glass causes it to vibrate. High and low sounds "vibrate" to produce sound. The volume of water in the glass will determine the speed of the vibration—and thus the pitch. The more water in the glass, the slower the vibrations and the deeper the tone.

PURPLE SLURPLE

God invites us to be members of his royal family. Let the "purple slurple" reign supreme!

Truth Explosion: Because God rules, we can be children of the King.

GODPRINT:
Integrity

TIME:
30 minutes

GROUP SIZE:
Small groups

MESS METER
1 2 **3**

In many countries, purple is the color of royalty. Let's make some very cool "purple slurple" to celebrate the fact that God invites us to be members of his royal family.

Combine 8 ounces of glue and 3/4 cup water in a bowl. **In Bible times, God was the first king of his people. Later he chose kings for them and promised that his kingdom would last forever. We can be members of God's royal family through faith.** Have kids stir in the "royal" purple Kool-Aid powder.

Now I need you scientists to start something new in another bowl. Have kids mix four tablespoons of borax with one cup of water in a second bowl. **The faith integrity of God's people long ago is passed on to God's people today to make a kingdom that lasts forever, mixed, blended and shaped by God's love.**

Let's put our two mixtures together and see what we get! Let kids add the borax mixture to the glue mixture and mix well. A wet, gooey clump will

FORMULA *for success*
- grape Kool-Aid® packet (.14 oz)
- white glue
- borax laundry powder
- mixing bowls/spoons
- zip-top snack bags
- measuring items

form. Remove the clump and knead it for about 15 minutes. Keep at it! The more the mixture is squeezed, the smoother the final product will be.

Hand out zip-top bags and let each child take a lump of purple slurple. Remind kids to keep their slurple stored in the bag when not in use. **Let this royal mix remind you that you're a member of the best-named family of all— the family of believers in Christ.**

Lab Results

• Sniff your slurple. How does the sweet smell remind you of how God's people add "fragrance" to today's world?
• Shape your slurple into a little person. How is God shaping your life?
• What's the best part of being a member of God's royal family?

Let's always remember to make faith choices that demonstrate that we are new creations in Christ Jesus.

USE THIS SCIENCE ACTIVITY WITH:

• Nicodemus learns about being born again. John 3:1–17 (*Nicodemus, a Pharisee, came by night and learned from Jesus about a new life in God.*)
• Zacchaeus finds a new life. Luke 19:1–10 (*Zacchaeus, a greedy tax collector, chose to show the sincerity of his new life by giving back more than he had taken.*)

To all who received him, to those who believed in his name, he gave the right to become children of God—children born not of natural descent nor of human decision... but born of God.

John 1:12, 13

EARTH SCIENCE

Get ready for a little mess and a tub-o-fun as your kids make miniature rivers that flow downhill.

Truth Explosion: God can do amazing things. I can trust him.

GODPRINT:
Trust

TIME:
35 minutes

GROUP SIZE:
Groups of 4 or 5

MESS METER

1 2 **3**

God can do amazing things. No one else can create the world and the rivers in it. God has power even over nature, and he uses that power for our good. We can trust him.

Make a river in a plastic tub. Gather supplies for as many groups of four or five as you anticipate. If you have outdoor space for this activity, take advantage of it.

Pile stones of different sizes at one end of a plastic tub to form a hill. Then cover the stones with soil. (For a less messy option, you can cover the stones with a plastic garbage bag.) Press the soil against the stones and shape it so you have a hill sloping down to the opposite edge of the tub. Add some stones on the side of the hill on top of the dirt.

Stand at the hill end of the tub and pour water over the hill. Watch as the water becomes a little river carrying dirt downhill. Make sure everyone has an opportunity to pour water down the hill. Add more stones and dirt as necessary if the hill erodes too much. Invite others to try to stop the river from flowing down the hill.

> ## FORMULA
> *for success*
> - plastic tubs
> - potting soil
>   - stones
>   - water
> - Optional: plastic garbage bag

Lab Results

• Let's name some of the biggest, mightiest rivers we can think of. *(Kids may mention Nile, Amazon, Mississippi or others they have learned about in school.)*

• When you stand on the banks of a river, or see some great pictures of one, how does that make you feel about God?

• The same God who created the amazing rivers of the world cares for you. How does knowing that make it easier to face tough situations?

He will rule from sea to sea and from the River to the ends of the earth.

Psalm 72:8

SUPER Science facts

Water's weight changes the surface of the Earth. Channels of water will eventually erode the surface underneath it, a process known as water weight erosion.

USE THIS SCIENCE ACTIVITY WITH:

• Crossing the Red Sea. Exodus 14:5–31 *(Moses trusted God as he led his people across the dry ground of the Red Sea.)*

• Crossing the Jordan. Joshua 3:1–17. *(God provided a miracle and led the people safely across the Jordan River.)*

• Naaman dips in the Jordan and is healed. 2 Kings 5:1–27 *(Naaman learned that the power to heal his leprosy was not in the dirty river water, but in God's care for him.)*

THERE GOES THE EGG!

Godly choices take your kids back to God. Eggs-actly!

Truth Explosion: God loves me no matter what. I can always come back to him.

GODPRINT:
Responsibility

TIME:
5–10 minutes

GROUP SIZE:
Individual or pairs

MESS METER
1 **2** 3

USE THIS SCIENCE ACTIVITY WITH:

- King Saul sacrificed wrongly. 1 Samuel 13. *(The prophet Samuel held Saul accountable for his wrong choice.)*
- The Parable of the Prodigal Son. Luke 15:11–32 *(The repentant son took responsibility for his poor choices.)*
- Zacchaeus meets Jesus. Luke 19:2–10 *(Zacchaeus took responsibility for what he had done wrong and made restitution.)*

Check the fire codes and sprinkler systems in your building before lighting matches. Use the marker to write "Me" on one bottle and "Godly Choice" on the other.

Set a peeled, boiled egg on top of the "Me" bottle. Try to gently push the egg into the bottle. Let several kids try. Finally have one student try really hard and squish the egg into the bottle. **What a mess! We know that when we make poor choices we end up with a mess we're sorry for later.**

FORMULA *for success*
- boiled eggs
- matches
- glass bottles with a 1 1/2 inch opening (coffee drink bottles work well)
- permanent marker
- wooden skewer

Set an egg on the "Godly Choices" bottle. **How about a fresh start? God is always ready to welcome us back with loving arms.** Light three matches, then quickly lift the egg on the "Godly Choices" bottle, drop the matches into the bottle and quickly replace the egg. The egg will be sucked into the bottle. **God's love draws us back to him!** Use the skewer to chop and remove the egg. Have kids give the experiment a try.

Lab Results

- What poor choices do kids make in order to "fit in," much like the egg in our experiment? How are they hurt and bruised in the process?
- Plan a party! Think of ways to celebrate "coming home"—back to God.

Do not be foolish, but understand what the Lord's will is.

Ephesians 5:17

SALT AND WATER PRAYERS

Does God stick? Assure your kids...every time!

Truth Explosion: We are drawn to pray and serve God.

Before class, lay the tablecloth on the table and cut 12-inch lengths of threads, one for each student. Scatter ice cubes on the table.

God hears and answers our prayers. Not because we remembered to pray this morning or because we never miss church, but because God loves us. God sticks with us!

> **FORMULA** *for success*
> - ice cubes
> - thread
> - salt shaker
> - small container of water
> - lined tablecloth

Moisten the threads. **Now drop your thread onto one of the ice cubes. Try to form a circle with the thread and pick up the ice cube.** (Obviously, this will not work). **Hmm. Let this remind us that without prayer we can't conquer heartbreak or handle life's struggles.**

Ask your kids to once again coil the wet end of their threads onto the ice cubes. This time shake a little salt on the cubes and wait 10 minutes. **Now try and lift the cube.** *(Fun Science Fact: Salt lowers the freezing point of water. As the water refreezes, the ice traps the string.)* The cube should lift and stay suspended from the thread. **God answers prayer. Pray, pray, pray!**

Lab Results
- Name a time when prayer helped you face an impossible situation.

Be alert and always keep on praying for all the saints.
Ephesians 6:18

GODPRINT:
Prayerfulness

TIME:
10 minutes

GROUP SIZE:
Individual or pairs

MESS METER
1 **2** 3

USE THIS SCIENCE ACTIVITY WITH:

- Jesus teaches us how to pray. Luke 11:1–4 *(The disciples asked Jesus to teach them to pray.)*

- The church prays for Peter's release. Acts 12:5–17 *(God heard the prayers of the people and freed Peter from prison.)*

- Daniel in the lions' den. Daniel 6:1–28 *(Prayer landed Daniel in a lions' den, but he didn't stop.)*

- The centurion asks Jesus to heal his servant. Matthew 8:5–13 *(The centurion knew that Jesus had the supernatural power to answer his request.)*

NOW YOU FEEL IT! NOW YOU DON'T!

Icky, sticky stuff and loving choices? Sure thing!

Truth Explosion: God blesses us when we make loving choices.

Form "Goop Groups" of three to four kids. **Let's see how touch changes this mixture we're about to make.**

• Place 1 cup warm water in the mixing bowl.
• Add 1 to 1 1/2 cups cornstarch. (The room's humidity will determine the right mix of cornstarch to water.)
• Stir with your hands.

Amazing but true! When the mixture is allowed to sit, it is solid to the touch, but when it's scooped up, it becomes liquid and flows off the fingertips. **God's loving touch changes lives. We can choose to make loving choices, too**. (*Fun Science Fact: The starch molecules in the cornstarch are large compared to the water molecules. How the molecules "mix and mingle" determines how the mixture behaves, more like a liquid or more like a solid.*)

FORMULA for success
• cornstarch
• warm water
• measuring cups
• medium-sized mixing bowls
• Optional: plastic strawberry basket or slotted spoon for scooping the goop!

Lab Results
• How does your touch change the mixture?
• Have you ever seen a life changed by someone's loving touch?
• How can God's love flow from your hands into someone else's life?

Dear children, let us not love with words or tongue but with actions and in truth.

1 John 3:18

GODPRINT:
Love

TIME:
10–15 minutes

GROUP SIZE:
Groups of three or four

MESS METER
1 2 **3**

USE THIS SCIENCE ACTIVITY WITH:

• Ruth shows her love for Naomi. Ruth 1:1–4:12 (*Ruth's loving touch made all the difference in Naomi's life.*)

• Joseph and Mary. Matthew 1:18–25; Luke 1:26–38; 2:1–7 (*Joseph lovingly followed God's direction and did not abandon Mary.*)

• Parable of the Prodigal Son. Luke 15:11–32 (*Jesus gives us a picture of a loving God.*)

• The gift of love. 1 Corinthians 13 (*Paul teaches on the supremacy of love in relationships.*)

VOLCANO THUNDER

Kaboom! Hear the sound of thunder and feel the earth shake (well, just a little!) as your kids follow the commandments of the one, true God.

Truth Explosion: We worship God and submit to his authority.

When God spoke to Moses about the Ten Commandments, the Israelites could see smoke, fire and lightning on Mount Sinai. Let's create a smoking mountain. It will help us remember that God wants our full attention as well as our submission and obedience to his laws.

Place the jars on top of the trays and fill them halfway with water. If you wish, let kids make a realistic-looking mountain by piling stones around the jar or wrapping it with a wide-mouth cone cut from fine-grade sandpaper. Have kids add a teaspoon of baking soda and stir it with straws until it dissolves completely. Add the detergent and a few drops of red food coloring. Slowly pour a 1/3 cup of vinegar into each jar and watch the foamy special effects!

Lab Results

• Why did God take time to give laws to his people?
• What happens when people ignore God's laws?

Come, let us bow down in worship, let us kneel before the Lord our Maker.

Psalm 95:6

FORMULA for success

• baby food jars
• water
• white vinegar
• 1 tsp. of baking soda (per student)
• 1 tsp. of laundry detergent (per student)
• straws
• trays or protective tablecloth
• Optional: small stones or fine-grade sandpaper, a few drops of red food coloring

GODPRINT:
Submissiveness

TIME:
35 minutes

GROUP SIZE:
Group project

MESS METER

1 2 **3**

USE THIS SCIENCE ACTIVITY WITH:

• Moses and the Israelites receive the Ten Commandments from God. Exodus 19:1–8; 20:1–11 (*God tells his people what choices please him.*)

• Josiah cleans the temple and renews the covenant. 2 Kings 22:1–13; 23:1–6; 23:21–23 (*Josiah led the people back to God's Word.*)

• Jesus submits to God's will in the garden. John 17:1–18:11 (*Jesus submits to God's will.*)

A CHIP OFF THE OLD BLOCK

Allow this simple activity to teach a point on perseverance.

GODPRINT:
Perseverance

TIME:
5 minutes

GROUP SIZE:
Individual

MESS METER

1 2 3

USE THIS SCIENCE ACTIVITY WITH:

• Joseph commits to be part of God's plan. Matthew 1:18–2:15 *(Joseph persevered and did what God asked him to do.)*

• Elijah confronts King Ahab on Mt. Carmel. 1 Kings 18:1–39 *(Even though he was outnumbered 400 to 1, Elijah didn't back down from doing what God asked him to do.)*

• Nehemiah leads the people in rebuilding Jerusalem. Nehemiah 6–8 *(Nehemiah faced many obstacles in rebuilding the wall but stuck with it.)*

Truth Explosion: God gives me the strength to do his will.

Pass out napkins, cookies and toothpicks.

Determination gets us through the day-to-day jobs in life. Another word for determination is perseverance. Where would we be without it! Think of a lifeguard who decides she really doesn't feel like rescuing anybody today. Or a construction crew who starts a bridge only to decide there's enough bridges in the world—and quits! In the same way, we, too, need perseverance to see us through God's plan.

FORMULA *for success*
• chocolate chip cookies
• toothpicks
• two or three toothbrushes
• napkins

Pick up a cookie and a toothpick. **Your archeological job: Try to remove** *whole* **chocolate chips from your cookie by using only a toothpick. You may scratch, pick and scrape it, but you cannot break the cookie. Keep at it and let's see how successful you are!** Have kids use toothbrushes to brush away crumbs. Have extra cookies on hand for munching.

Lab Results

• How is this activity a lot like the struggles we have in living a godly life?
• Perseverance means sticking to it until you get the job done. How did Jesus persevere in his Father's plan for his life?

A righteous man may have many troubles, but the LORD delivers him from them all.

Psalm 34:19

POP! POP! POP!

Give your kids a rock poppin' surprise while everyone praises the King of kings.

Truth Explosion: Jesus is the King of kings and Lord or lords. Even rocks shout his praise!

Let kids open a packet of the candy.

The crowds praised Jesus as he entered Jerusalem. They could hardly contain themselves! Here was the "man of miracles," who had been teaching and healing around the countryside for three years. Jesus tells us that rocks would sing his praises even if the people didn't.

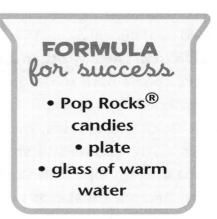

FORMULA *for success*

- Pop Rocks® candies
- plate
- glass of warm water

Pour some warm water into a plate.

Jesus is the master of all creation. Some of the people in the crowd understood that, but many of them didn't. Today, from this side of the Resurrection, we know that Jesus is the King of kings. We have some small, colorful rocks here. On the count of three, let's drop these "rocks" into the water and see what happens. Have kids stand back. The candy will "cry out" with fizzles and pops in all directions!

Lab Results

- Why did Jesus say if people didn't praise him, the stones would cry out?
- Why do you think the religious leaders wanted to hush the crowds?
- What is the most natural way for you to praise Jesus?

Worship the LORD with gladness; come before him with joyful songs.

Psalm 100:2

GODPRINT:
Worship

TIME:
Less than 2 minutes!

GROUP SIZE:
Pairs or as one large group

MESS METER
1 2 **3**

USE THIS SCIENCE ACTIVITY WITH:

- The people praise Jesus as king. Luke 19:29–40 (*As Jesus entered Jerusalem, the adoring crowd shouted his praises.*)

- The shepherds worship Jesus. Luke 2:8–20 (*The angels showed the shepherds how to worship, and the shepherds went quickly to Bethlehem to worship.*)

- Mary anoints Jesus with perfume. Matthew 26:6–13 (*Mary gave the best she had in an act of personal worship.*)

HE HAS RISEN

Watch shirt buttons rise to the surface as your kids hear of Jesus' resurrection from the grave.

Truth Explosion: God gives us hope through his Son, Jesus Christ.

GODPRINT:
Hope

TIME:
5 minutes

GROUP SIZE:
Individual or pairs

MESS METER
1 2 3

Hand each student a cup. **In many ways Jesus was a man like any other. As he carried his cross up the road to Golgotha, his beaten body cried out for water.** Pour soda into each cup. **Once there, Jesus, the "living water"** (John 4:10), **obediently stretched out his arms and lay upon the cross. Nail holes soon pierced his hands and feet.** Pass out buttons. Have students use their fingertips to feel the four holes on the button's surface.

FORMULA
for success
- clear, carbonated beverage
- 4-hole buttons
- clear plastic cups

The chief priests, the teachers of the law, the elders and the common people crowded around the cross and hurled insults at Jesus. Jesus heard it all. With one last cry, Jesus gave up his spirit. Drop the buttons into the soda.

Early on the first day of the week, Mary Magdalene went to the tomb to care for Jesus' body. The tomb was empty. Watch closely as the carbonated bubbles attach to the buttons. Quickly, the buttons rise to the surface. **Jesus had risen. He rose from the dead just as he said he would!** Tap the cup to dislodge the gas bubbles so the button will sink—and rise—again.

Lab Results

• How was Jesus' rising from the dead a lot like what our buttons did? *(People were shocked and surprised that Jesus would indeed rise again.)*

• In your own words, how does God give us hope through his Son?

• When could you demonstrate this science and share your hope in Jesus with your family?

The risen Jesus is all the hope we need to live our lives for him.

Thanks be to God! He gives us the victory through our Lord Jesus Christ.

1 Corinthians 15:57

SUPER
Science facts

Carbon dioxide bubbles give soda its fizz. When the bubbles cling to the button, it gives it buoyancy or lift and the button rises.

USE THIS SCIENCE ACTIVITY WITH:

• Jesus dies; Peter finds the empty tomb. Matthew 27:33–54; John 20:1–8 *(When Peter saw the empty tomb and the grave clothes, he knew that Jesus was victorious over death.)*

Substitute raisins or mothballs for the buttons for the following stories.

• Jesus raises Jairus' daughter. Luke 8:40–42, 49–56. *(Jesus shows the hope God brings by raising a girl from the dead.)*

• Friends bring a paralytic to Jesus. Mark 2:3–12 *(Four friends had hope that Jesus could help.)*

• Lazarus is raised from the dead. John 11:1–44 *(Jesus showed the power of God over death when his friend returned to life.)*

BLOW ME OVER HOPE

Pair feelings of hopelessness with that of compassion. Allow your kids to see how one needs the caring action of the other.

Truth Explosion: Because Jesus helps even when things seem hopeless, I can show I care.

GODPRINT:

Hope

TIME:

15 minutes

GROUP SIZE:

Individual

MESS METER

1 2 3

"Take your time."
"Time stands still."
"I don't have time."
"Time's up."

We have 101 expressions about time—something that we can't feel or hold in our hands.

For example, do you get a little nervous when it's time to go to school and you can't find your shoes, backpack, homework or lunch money? As we all know, school buses wait for no one! And do your parents make it worse when they ask you to make up time and get moving?

Have volunteers share times that leave them pressured, discouraged and overwhelmed.

Pass out the index cards. **Now it's your turn! On your card write or draw a time that is an everyday discouragement, one that makes you feel at odds with the world. Maybe it's getting up in the morning, doing your math homework or facing a sink full of greasy dishes.** Allow kids to draw or write. Go ahead and pick up a pencil and make a drawing of your own. **Now flip the card and draw or write your favorite time of day—time filled** with relaxation and the feeling that you have "all the time in the world." When kids finish, demonstrate how to gently bend the index card and set it on the table. Make sure the discouraging side faces out.

Now try to flip your card by blowing on it. This may look easy, but it's not. Even when kids blow above or below the card, the card should not flip.

So sorry! I set you up for that. I knew it was hopeless, but I did it to prove a point. Can anyone tell me what that is? Very good! When we or those around us feel hopeless, Jesus can help. Always.

Lab Results
• What do you do when you feel hopeless? What makes you feel better?
• How can Jesus help you when things seem hopeless?
• How can you give hope to someone else by sharing the love of Jesus?

Jesus healed a lot of people when it seemed hopeless—even raising some from the dead. We can show others we care by sharing the hope that comes from knowing our Savior.

You, **O Lord, are a compassionate and gracious God, slow to anger, abounding in love and faithfulness.**

Psalm 86:15

USE THIS SCIENCE ACTIVITY WITH:
• Jesus raises Jairus's daughter from the dead. Luke 8:40–42, 49–56 (*Friends and relatives had given up hope until Jesus performed a compassionate miracle.*)

• The Good Samaritan. Luke 10:25–37 (*Compassion came from an unexpected source.*)

• Jesus heals ten men with leprosy. Luke 17:11–19 (*Jesus' compassion gave the ten men new hope.*)

• Jesus heals a man at the pool of Bethesda. John 5:1–15 (*Jesus shows compassion for a man who could not act in his own strength.*)

EFFERVESCENT FOLKS

Kids love to see things take off. Use this activity to help them take off with praise.

Truth Explosion: God alone is worthy of our highest honor, attention and praise.

GODPRINT:

Worship

TIME:

20 minutes

GROUP SIZE:

Individual or pairs

MESS METER

1 2 **3**

Make sure to launch a "Zip-Zop Praise Rocket" before class to see how it operates. Refill it and have it on hand to show your kids. Remember to lay down your tablecloth launch pad before lift off begins.

Zip-Zop Praise Rockets will remind us to praise and worship Jesus, our Savior. Have each student make a five-inch wide construction paper tube to fit around the film canister. **Face the open end of the canister downward and make sure it sticks out about 1/8 inch from the bottom of the tube. Securely tape the construction paper tube to the canister. Then cut and accordion fold construction paper arms and feet and tape them to your tube. Hands reaching upward would be an appropriate posture for worship!**

Pause as kids work. Then hold up a canister lid. **Make a little loop of tape, sticky side out, and put it on the inside of the canister lid. Now stick the seltzer tablet to the tape.**

Show kids how to pour a little bit of water into the canister—about 1/4 full. Line the kids up for a group launch or let them take turns. When each rocket is ready to launch, snap on the lid (with the attached seltzer tablet). Quickly turn the

FORMULA for success

- film canisters with snap-on lids
- construction paper
- scissors
- clear tape
- effervescent (fizzing) antacid tablets
- pitcher of water
- plastic tablecloth for a launch pad

rocket over and set it on the launching pad. Stand back. Zip-Zop Praise Rockets will zip-zop pop in powerful praise!

Lab Results

• What made our little praise rockets really take off? (*They were bubbling inside and the bubbles had to escape.*)

• How is worship and praise like all those excited bubbles? (*If we get excited about God, we can't help but worship him and tell others.*)

• When can you make Zip-zop Praise Rockets at home?

There is no one else like God! He's the only one worthy of our highest honor, attention and praise.

Worship the Lord your God and serve him only.

Luke 4:8

SUPER Science facts

When the effervescent tablet and water mix, gas pressure builds inside the film canister. When enough pressure builds the canister blows its top!

USE THIS SCIENCE ACTIVITY WITH:

• The shepherds worship Jesus. Luke 2:1–20 (*The shepherds heard the angels worship, then hurried to Bethlehem to worship Jesus too.*)

• The wise men worship Jesus. Matthew 2:1–12 (*The wise men traveled a long way to worship Jesus.*)

• God creates the world. Genesis 1:1–24 (*We respond to God's awesome creation when we worship him as Creator.*)

• The people praise Jesus as king. Luke 19:29–39 (*Jesus rode into Jerusalem as a king; the people worshiped him because he came in the name of the Lord.*)

MAKE NO MISTAKE

Kids will make a few mistakes in this activity—until they learn God's way of doing things.

Truth Explosion: God can change anyone's heart.

GODPRINT:

Commitment

TIME:

10 minutes

GROUP SIZE:

Individual

MESS METER

1 2 3

Hand out the paper strips and the markers, one strip and marker per student. Make sure to keep a paper strip and marker for yourself.

Use your marker to draw a heart on your paper strip. Pause. **That's great. Now on the other side of your strip, write or draw a common mistake that kids your age do that makes life harder for others.** (A few examples: gossip, disobeying parents, cheating, lying.)

FORMULA
for success
- markers
- strips of paper
- table

Now place your paper strip close to the edge of the table like this. Demonstrate for your kids using your paper strip and marker.

Then stand the marker, which represents you, near the paper's edge. The object is to see if you can pull out the paper strip, filled with mistakes, without knocking "yourself" (the marker) over in the process. Rule #1: You can use both hands but you may not touch the marker. Kids will try various methods but markers will undoubtedly tilt and fall.

We all have mistakes written in our hearts. We can try and try but we can't keep them from tipping us over. But in Jesus we become new creations—forgiven of our bad deeds and harmful attitudes and ready to spread God's Word.

Set markers on top of the paper slips again. **Let's try this a whole new way. God's way! Hold the end of the paper slip gently in one hand and use the pointer finger on your other hand to give it a swift chop just in front of the marker**. This time the markers should stay upright! You may want to practice this a couple of times before class to get it right the first time.

Lab Results

• How do the mistakes we make tip us over the way our markers fell over?

• What happens to mistakes when Jesus comes into our life? *(We still make mistakes, but God forgives us; we try to be more and more like Jesus.)*

• How have you seen God at work in your life making you a "new creation"?

God can change hearts. We won't suddenly be perfect, but we'll have God's help with the choices we make in the future. It's a whole new starting point, make no mistake about it!

If anyone is in Christ, he is a new creation; the old has gone the new has come!
2 Corinthians 5:17

USE THIS SCIENCE ACTIVITY WITH:

• Saul is converted and becomes a missionary. Acts 9:1–28, 13:1–3 *(Paul worked against the Christians, but God changed Paul's heart. Paul committed his life to serve Christ.)*

• Zacchaeus. Luke 19:1–10 *(Zacchaeus was a hated tax collector who had stolen from the people. When he met Jesus he changed and committed to give back more than he had taken.)*

• Paul and the Philippian jailer. Acts 16:16–40 *(Paul helped the Roman jailer believe in Jesus. The jailer's whole family began to serve God.)*

CHOICES, CHOICES

Can your kids stand the pressure? Make simple pencil holders and discuss the benefits of wise choices.

Truth Explosion: Because God is wise, I can make wise choices.

Hand out sheets of paper and pencils for kids to use.

GODPRINT:

Wisdom

TIME:

20 minutes

GROUP SIZE:

Individual

MESS METER

1 2 3

Let's get right to the point (hold up your pencil) **of our lesson today. Pick up your paper and see if you can stand it in such a way that it will hold your pencil. In other words, make your plain sheet of paper into a pencil holder!** Allow kids a minute or two to work. Undoubtedly, you'll have kids who will bend and shape their papers to fashion one-of-a-kind pencil holders. Good for them!

FORMULA
for success
- plain paper
- pencils
- small classroom items such as glue sticks, small jars, hole puncher, scissors, paperback books, erasers

Good thinking. As we discovered, paper without any folds cannot take the weight or pressure of even a simple pencil. Without our wise God, we, too, cannot stand up for what we believe in and make wise choices.

For those kids who haven't figured it out yet show them how to fold the paper in half lengthwise. Then starting at the short end, accordion fold the paper. *(Fun Science Fact: This paper stand is surprisingly sturdy. As origami enthusiasts know, folded paper derives its strength from its structure and construction.)*

Now place your pencil holder on the table and place your pencil proudly on top! **Allow it to remind you to make a stand for God—a wise choice guaranteed!**

Have kids pair up. Set out the small classroom items. **Take turns with your partner and talk about the peer pressure you face on the playground or on the bus after school. How well do you stand up? As you share stories, pick an object and place it on your "pencil holder." See if it can take the pressure.**

Lab Results

• What kinds of things do friends say that hurt your feelings?

• In what ways do friends help you make wise choices? In what ways do friends make it harder to make wise choices?

• If God hired you to manufacture a gizmo that would help kids resist peer pressure what would it look or sound like?

It's not easy to know or make the right choice when the pressure's on. The good news is we don't have to rely on our own strength or wisdom. We can rely on God to make wise choices.

For the LORD gives wisdom, and from his mouth come knowledge and understanding.

Proverbs 2:6

USE THIS SCIENCE ACTIVITY WITH:

• Daniel and friends stand up for their beliefs. Daniel 1:1–20. (*The young men did not give in to peer pressure or the wishes of a very powerful king.*

• Abraham makes a wise choice for peace. Genesis 13:1–17. (*Abraham made a wise choice for peace.*)

• Caleb and Joshua stand up for God's power. Numbers 13:1–2, 17–30; 14:6–9 (*Ten spies pressured Caleb and Joshua, but both made the wise choice to believe God's promise and power.*)

HOPE THAT SOARS

Oops! Unexpected trouble turns into a lesson on hope that never grows faint.

Truth Explosion: Because God's love for me is forever, I can be hopeful even when unexpected things happen.

GODPRINT:

Hope

TIME:

10 minutes

GROUP SIZE:

Small

MESS METER

1 2 3

Welcome each of your kids with a balloon. Set out a balloon, a pen and an empty 2-liter bottle for you to use in today's experiment.

• What things made your week hopeful or "struggle-ful?"
• Anyone wish to share a major disappointment?

Today let's talk about hope. Take your ballpoint pen and draw a smiley face on your balloon. Blow it up. **And unexpected troubles!** Release the air from the balloon. **Who's up for a little unexpected trouble?**

Go ahead and prove to me how easy it is to blow up an ordinary balloon. Allow kids to stretch and blow up their balloons.

We're learning today that because God's love is forever, we can be light and hopeful—just like a balloon—even when unexpected things rattle our day. Insert the base of your deflated balloon into the empty 2-liter bottle. Invert the mouthpiece over the bottle opening (see diagram) and blow into the bottle. Blow harder! You will not be able to blow up the balloon completely. **Whew! This is hard. When the pressure builds up there's no telling what'll happen! I think I'm losing hope.** Pass around the extra 2-liter bottles you brought to class. Have your kids take turns inserting their balloons to try and blow them up. **No fainting, please!**

FORMULA for success

- balloons
- ballpoint pen
- empty and clean 2-liter bottle(s)
- empty and clean peanut butter jar(s)

After a while, collect the bottles. **Pressure schmessure! Isaiah 40:31 tells us that hope is our gift from God. We will not grow weary in his care. Or faint!** Hold up the peanut butter jar. If your smiley balloon is still useful, hold it up too. **Okay. Let's give this one more try. Let's think. How can I pick up this empty jar with my stretched-out-and tired-yet-still-hopeful little-balloon?** Listen to guesses.

You got it! Place the jar on a table. Hold the deflated balloon inside the jar. Lean over and blow the balloon up. The balloon will quickly fill the insides of the jar. Stand up. The jar will lift off the table. Have kids give it a try with their balloons.

Lab Results

• What kinds of things do you hope for?
• How does remembering God's care for you help you be hopeful?

Unexpected things pop up, and we get disappointed or frustrated. But hope surprises us, too. Just when things seem impossible, God shows the way with hope that soars on air.

USE THIS SCIENCE ACTIVITY WITH:

• Job's trials. Job 1:1–22; 2:7–10; 42:1, 2, 10–13 *(If anyone had reason to feel hopeless, it was Job. But he never gave up and hoped in God.)*

• God speaks to Elijah with a gentle whisper. 1 Kings 19:1–18 *(Elijah was tired of trying to help people who wouldn't listen to him. God gave him hope.)*

• Paul and Silas in Prison. Acts 16:16–40 *(Paul and Silas were out of options until God sent an earthquake that broke their prison chains and changed a jailer's heart forever.)*

Those who hope in the Lord will renew their strength. They will soar on wings like eagles; they will run and not grow weary, they will walk and not be faint.

Isaiah 40:31

SUPER Science facts

As the air pressure inside the balloon increases so does the air pressure trapped inside the bottle. This balance of pressure and counter-pressure is so strong that no amount of breath can overcome it.

HUMILITY ON THE RISE

See humility in your kids without lifting a finger!

Truth Explosion: Because Jesus humbled himself, he helps me think of others before myself.

If you have a large class, prepare several sets of supplies so everyone can have a close look.

GODPRINT:
Humility

TIME:
15 minutes

GROUP SIZE:
Whole class or small groups

MESS METER

1 2 3

FORMULA
for success
• brightly colored golf ball
• smiley sticker
• uncooked rice
• wide-mouth jar with lid

When is it difficult for you to place the needs of others before your own? *(When I'd rather be playing on the computer or eating a snack; when kids are mean or selfish to me.)*

Have kids gather around you as you set the jar on a table. Place the smiley sticker on the golf ball and then gently place the ball inside the jar. **Hello, Mr. Humility! Mr. Humility reminds us that when we humble ourselves we think of others first.** Have students take turns pouring small amounts of dry rice on top of the golf ball. Keep adding rice until the ball is covered by three inches or more. Be sure to allow 1 1/2 inches of space at the top of the jar.

Screw on the jar lid. Ask a volunteer to hold the jar and move or "stir" it from side to side (not up and down) without lifting it from the table. **Watch what happens!** In no time, the golf ball rises and rests neatly on the surface of the rice. Remove the lid.

Without lifting a finger...I mean, the jar...we saw Mr. Humility rise above the busyness and frustrations of his own life to willingly serve others—all with a smile!

Repeat the experiment until everyone has a chance to try it.

Lab results

• What example of humility does Jesus give us? *(He humbled himself enough to die for us.)*

• Name two ways you could humble yourself at home? *(Choose a household job that no one likes to do—clean the kitty litter box and do it without complaint; agree to shower last on a school morning; read to a younger brother even if you're just dying to lace up your soccer spikes and head for the field!)*

• How does a humble attitude show brothers and sisters, family and friends that you care?

Jesus humbled himself when he came to earth to live. Although divine and holy and without sin, he humbled himself and died on a cross. In his humility, Jesus showed how much he cared for you and me.

Each of you should look not only to your own interests, but also to the interests of others.

Philippians 2:4

USE THIS SCIENCE ACTIVITY WITH:

• Jesus' example of humility. Philippians 2:1–11 *(By dying for us, Jesus gives us the supreme example of thinking of others instead of himself.)*

• Parable of the place of honor. Luke 14:1–14 *(Jesus teaches that we should be humble and think of others before ourselves.)*

• Jesus washes the disciples' feet. John 13:1–17 *(Jesus shows humility by doing the task of a servant.)*

SUPER Science facts

Two things cannot occupy the same space at the same time. Shaking or stirring the jar forces the grains of rice closer together. This pressure pushes the golf ball to the surface.

NOT SOLD SEPARATELY

Captivate your kids with swirling color. Use this activity to teach a lesson on compassion.

Truth Explosion: Because Jesus shows compassion, I can show I care.

GODPRINT:

Compassion

TIME:

10 minutes

GROUP SIZE:

Large group

MESS METER

1 2 3

FORMULA *for success*
- a glass filled with water
- powdered fruit drinks (cherry, lime and grape)
- spoons
- Optional: food coloring, bowl, cup, cooking oil

Greetings to my favorite bunch of kids. Let's mix a little color today! Place the water-filled glass and powdered fruit drinks where kids can reach. If you wish, substitute food coloring for the powdered fruit drink mixes.

Ask volunteers to use the flat handle of the spoons and scoop up some of the powdered fruit drink and pour it into the glass, one color at a time.

Work slowly, dropping the colors from a height of two inches or more above the rim. *(Fun Science Fact: The added height causes each color to precipitate (or fall) deeper into the glass.)* Watch as colors spread throughout the water eventually blending together.

After awhile, say, **Oh no. I wanted to do this for the class next door, too. Quick. Help me, _____(fill in with a student's name), grab the colors and put them back into the packages. Hurry, please. I can't be late!**

Your kids will look at you like you have two heads. Go with it!

After the looks pass, smile. **Clearly it's impossible to separate colors once they've mixed. And aren't mixed up days a lot like that? Sometimes we feel like nobody cares and nothing we do will make things better. We started the day a sunny yellow! But somehow it ended up faded and washed out.**

Allow a few minutes for kids to share their thoughts and feelings on mixed up days.

On such days, a hug and smile from a compassionate friend makes things better and brighter. It's also the time for us to remember that nothing, even faded days, can separate us from the love of God. His compassion is easy to get a hold of—just open your Bible!

Lab Results
• Name some stories in the Bible where Jesus showed compassion.
• How does God's love turn things around on a gray day?

When we remember that we are never alone, we can show compassion for others who struggle with mixed up days, too!

Something Extra!
For another simple experiment in color, pour 1 tablespoon of cooking oil into a cup. Add three drops each of red, green and blue food colorings. Mix well. Pour the colored oil into a clear bowl of water. Beautiful! Streams of color appear throughout the bowl.

USE THIS SCIENCE ACTIVITY WITH:

• Jesus raises Jairus's daughter. Luke 8:40–42, 49–56 *(Jesus showed compassion for two parents heartbroken by the death of their daughter.)*

• Jesus cares for 5,000 people. Mark 6:30–40 *(Jesus responded compassionately to a crowd's need.)*

• Four friends bring a paralytic to Jesus. Mark 2:3–12 *(Compassionate friends prompted a miraculous healing.)*

For I am convinced that neither death nor life, neither angels nor demons, neither the present nor the future, nor any powers, neither height nor depth, nor anything else in all creation, will be able to separate us from the love of God that is in Christ Jesus our Lord.

Romans 8:38, 39

SUPER Science facts

Sugar crystals (the solute) break apart in water (the solvent). The combination of the two produces a homogeneous mixture known as a solution.

CATCH ME IF YOU CAN

With the drop of a pencil, kids will realize how easily confidence turns to doubt and how much they need Jesus to keep their confidence meter high.

Truth Explosion: Because Jesus is the Son of God, I can trust him with my doubts.

GODPRINT:

Confidence

TIME:

15 minutes

GROUP SIZE:

Pairs

MESS METER

1 2 3

Hello and welcome! Put on your thinking caps. Today I have a three-part question to start our time together.

Here's part one. How many of you think you could catch a pencil thrown from across the room—using one hand only? Oh, by the way, you're blindfolded. Pause and allow kids to respond. **Not much confidence here!**

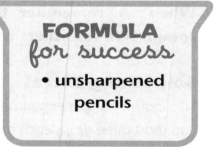

FORMULA *for success*

• unsharpened pencils

Okay. Part two. Suppose I give you permission to remove the blindfold. Could you catch the pencil now? Hmm. The confidence meter rises! Pause and allow kids to respond.

Now for part three. How many of you could catch a pencil if I held it right over your hand? *(No brainer!)* **Let's give it a try.** Have kids pair up. Pass out one unsharpened pencil for each pair of students. Grab a partner yourself and demonstrate the following action. Have your partner position his or her hand as if holding a glass. Hold the pencil 8 to 12 inches above your partner's hand. Have your kids follow your example.

On the count of three, drop your pencils.

(Fun Science Fact: By the time the eye sees the pencil fall and signals the brain, time is lost. Listen as confident pencils fall all over the place!) Switch roles. Some kids will do well with this activity and catch the pencil every time. Have those students decrease (and then increase) the distance between their pencils and hands.

Jesus knows better than we do our strengths and weaknesses. He also knows how quickly our confidence can tumble into doubt. The good news is—and there's so much of it in Jesus!—that Jesus helps us with our doubts.

Lab Results

• What kinds of things do you have the most doubts about? What helps to make you confident? Share some ways to show that you are confident in God.

Jesus will encourage our faith and give us confidence that he is the Son of God. Drop your doubts and catch his confidence!

Guide me in your truth and teach me, for you are God my Savior, and my hope is in you all day long.

Psalm 25:5

USE THIS SCIENCE ACTIVITY WITH:

• Jesus rises and appears to Thomas. John 19:1–18; 20:1–8, 19–31 *(Thomas discovered the meaning of confidence when Jesus appeared and invited him to explore the "proof" that he was alive.)*

• Peter walks on water to Jesus. Matthew 14:22–33 *(Peter walked on water until his confidence wavered.)*

• Jesus calms the storm for doubting disciples. Mark 4:35–41 *(The disciples were terrified. Jesus gave them a miraculous lesson on confidence in his power to control nature.)*

SUPER Science facts

Gravitation is the force of attraction that exists between all particles with mass in the universe. The force of gravity is responsible for holding objects onto the surface of planets.

SPREAD THE NEWS

Your kids will want to try this experiment for themselves as they learn about the amazing world God made.

Truth Explosion: Our Creator God made an amazing world. That includes us!

GODPRINT:

Wonder

TIME:

10 minutes

GROUP SIZE:

Large group

MESS METER

1 2 3

FORMULA
for success
- rulers
- table
- newspaper sheets

We live in a vast "sea" of air that exerts pressure around us and on our bodies all the time. Can you feel it? Shrug your shoulders freely and encourage the kids to do the same. Neither can I. Scientists have measured this pressure and found that our bodies can tolerate approximately 15 pounds of pressure for every square inch. Yet we don't feel it. God made our bodies so wonderfully that they adjust to this constant pressure naturally.

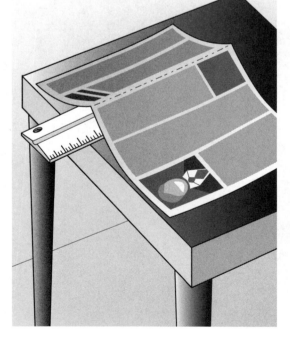

Use this easy method to prove the presence of air pressure. Place a ruler on a table so that one end hangs over the table's edge. Cover the remaining part with a single sheet of newspaper.

Point to the newspaper and ruler. **Talking about pressure, what do you think will happen to the newspaper if I put a great deal of pressure on the ruler's end? In other words, what if I went ahead and smacked the ruler's end with my fist?** *(Kids will speculate that the paper will tear or fly off because the other end of the ruler will come up.)*

Pause as kids respond. Then proceed with the experiment. Bring your fist sharply down on the free end of the ruler. Amazingly, the ruler will resist the blow of your fist. In fact, your strike may indeed snap the ruler without ever tearing or lifting the newspaper.

If you have extra rulers and newspaper, let kids try this activity for themselves.

Lab Results
• How did the results of this experiment compare with what you thought would happen?
• Name some other amazing things about the world God made.
• When you see the amazing way God created the world, what do you feel like saying to God?

Is it any wonder that God made an amazing world? And that includes you and me. You're amazing! I'm amazing! This same God who created the universe cares about our bodies and minds and souls.

Great is the LORD and most worthy of praise; his greatness no one can fathom.

Psalm 145:3

SUPER Science facts

The air pressure on the surface of the newspaper resists the sudden, upward force of the ruler. This causes the ruler to hold fast to the table.

USE THIS SCIENCE ACTIVITY WITH:
• God made the world. Genesis 1:1–2:2 *(We respond with wonder to the incredible world that God created for us.)*
• God has power over the sea. Mark 4:35–41 *(Our God of power and might cares for us!)*
• Jesus walks on water. Matthew 14:24–33 *(When we see God's power in action, we can't help but be amazed.)*

BODY BEAUTIFUL

Kids get an earful as they learn about the importance of listening to good advice.

Truth Explosion: God gives us wise people who freely share their good advice.

GODPRINT:

Discernment

TIME:

25 minutes

GROUP SIZE:

Small groups

MESS METER

1 **2** 3

We use our ears (*Fun Science Fact: ears are organs that detect vibratory motion*) **to hear a variety of vibrations. Bells, whistles, music, car engines, voices...**

• What noises do you hear on your way to school each day?

With so much going on, how well do we really hear? In other words, how well do we listen? There's an expression that sums up this thought nicely. Raise your ear if you've heard the expression—"in one ear and out the other?" Pause as kids try to raise their ears! **Exactly! It's as if our ears are stopped up and we can't hear what we need to hear.** Pass out the play dough. **I'd like you to use the play dough to sculpt an ear. Be sure to make it as large as possible because next you'll make earwax!**

Have kids work in groups for both the ears and the cornstarch "wax." Or you can measure ingredients for kids to make individual batches. The basic recipe is 1/2 cup of cornstarch and 1/4 cup of light corn syrup. Put these ingredients in the zip-top bag and add a few drops of water and yellow food coloring. Knead the bag to mix everything together. Multiply or divide the recipe as appropriate for your group. When everyone has a sculpted ear and a bag of "wax," distribute the cotton swabs.

FORMULA
for success
- play dough or soft clay
- zip-top bags
- cornstarch
- light corn syrup
- yellow food coloring
- water
- measuring cup
- cotton swabs

Hold up a sculpted ear. **Now suppose this ear is your ear. And you're in a situation where you need some wise advice. But the wise advice you hear means you can't do what you want or you have to do something very hard. Do you "tune out" and choose not to pay attention? Use your cotton swabs to fill your play dough ears with earwax.** As kids work have them share with their neighbors times when others "tune" them out and how that makes them feel.

Good vibrations equals good advice! When we refuse to listen to good advice, it's like we've stopped up our ears. But God sends us wise people who give us good advice. They're truly a blessing! So let's listen up and do our best to pay attention.

Lab Results

• Who can you trust to give you good advice in tough situations?

• What are some ways that you stop up your ears if you get advice that you really don't want to hear?

• How can we unstop our ears so that we can listen to good advice?

I have chosen the way of truth; I have set my heart on your laws.

Psalm 119:30

USE THIS SCIENCE ACTIVITY WITH:

• Rehoboam rejects the advice of elders. 1 Kings 12:1–19 *(Instead of listening to wise advise, King Rehoboam did what he wanted and divided a nation.)*

• Saul rejects Samuel's instructions and makes a sacrifice. 1 Samuel 13:1–15 *(Saul got impatient waiting for Samuel to arrive and took matters into his own hands, even though he knew it was wrong.)*

• Mordecai advises Esther and she saves her people. Esther 2:1–9:17 *(A fearful Esther listened to the good advice and helped save God's people.)*

MALLOWS OF PERFECT PEACE

Discover it's possible to be enthusiastic (and stress-free!) even when tackling hard tasks.

Truth Explosion: Because God is with me, I can work with confidence.

GODPRINT:

Enthusiasm

TIME:

15 minutes

GROUP SIZE:

Pairs

MESS METER

1 2 3

Twist your ear to make your tongue pop out. **I know what you're thinking. "That's easy. I can do that!"** Pause as kids try. **Okay. Now gently bend your thumb back so that it touches your wrist.** Pause. **Ouch! Now roll your tongue so that both sides touch each other. Finally, without closing either eye, find the tip of your nose. Still not easy? Remember, confidence in God helps us remain enthusiastic and stress-free when tackling hard tasks.**

FORMULA *for success*
- large marshmallows
- Optional: coins

USE THIS SCIENCE ACTIVITY WITH:

- God encourages Elijah with a gentle whisper. 1 Kings 19:1–18 *(Elijah lost his enthusiasm for God's work. God renewed it.)*
- Joseph dreams and is sold into slavery. Genesis 37:1–36 *(Joseph maintained his enthusiasm.)*
- Esther takes a risk. Esther 2:1–9:17 *(Despite her fears, Esther moves forward with a glad spirit.)*

Have kids try to catch marshmallows off their elbows. Demonstrate for the class by touching your shoulder with your hand. Make sure to point your elbow straight out in front of you. Now balance a marshmallow on the tip of your elbow. Pop up the marshmallow and swing your hand down (quickly) and catch it before it falls to the ground. Pass out the marshmallows and let kids give it a try. Challenge kids to stack marshmallows or try both elbows at once. For added fun, try coins.

Lab Results

• How did you feel about tackling something that turned out to be hard? *(Make sure you hear both from kids who mastered the trick and those who struggled.)* Why does God ask you to be enthusiastic?

You will keep in perfect peace him whose mind is steadfast, because he trusts in you.

Isaiah 26:3

POW-POW-POWER

Kids will find a new appreciation for God's loving power as they try to muster up their own power for a task that is not as simple as it seems.

Truth Explosion: Because Jesus uses his power in loving ways, I can ask him to help others.

Hand each student a balloon. Have kids blow up the balloons 1/2 to 3/4 full and knot them closed.

Let's get started with a bang. When I say "Pow," take your balloons and kneel on them. Hold up the bag of treats. **The first to burst his or her balloon with knee power wins the day and gets to hand out these powerfully tasty treats. Ready...set...POW!** Because the balloons are not blown to capacity, popping them will be difficult. *(Fun Science Fact: An underinflated balloon is protected from popping because of its flexible polymer skin.)* You may want to have the power of a pencil point handy to help pop the really tough cases.

Our physical power rules...sometimes. Let's name some powerful people whose power lies not in their muscles but in their wisdom, kindness, faith or prayerfulness. Allow kids to respond.

Lab Results
- Who are the people "in power" at school?
- What are some differences between physical and spiritual power?
- How do government representatives use their power?

If you remain in me and my words remain in you, ask whatever you wish, and it will be given you.

John 15:7

FORMULA for success
- balloons
- bag of treats
- sharpened pencil

GODPRINT:
Prayerfulness

TIME:
10 minutes

GROUP SIZE:
Individual

MESS METER
1 2 3

USE THIS SCIENCE ACTIVITY WITH:

- Jesus heals the centurion's servant. Matthew 8:5–13 *(The centurion asked boldly for Jesus' help)*

- Four friends bring a paralytic to Jesus. Mark 2:3–12 *(The friends knew that Jesus could help and did whatever they could to get their friend to Jesus.)*

- Jesus heals blind Bartimaeus. Mark 10:46–52; Luke 18:35–43 *(Bartimaeus didn't hesitate to ask for what he needed for himself.)*

A COLORFUL SPREAD

Let your kids see how fast they can spread the Good News while they watch swirling colors speed across a milky world.

GODPRINT:
Evangelism

TIME:
10 minutes

GROUP SIZE:
Groups of 4

MESS METER

1 2 3

Truth Explosion: When we receive the gift of salvation, God empowers us to carry on the work of his kingdom.

Jesus wants us to be his witnesses to the very ends of the earth. Point to the cake pans. **The round cake pans represent our round Earth. Let's see what we can do to spread the news of Jesus.**

FORMULA
for success
- round cake pans
- whole milk (warmed)
- food coloring
- dishwashing liquid

Gather kids in groups of four around the cake pans. Have kids pour milk into the cake pans to a 1-inch depth. **Choose a food color to represent "witnesses."** Let each group of students choose a color.

Take turns squeezing a drop of food coloring near the edge of the pan.

Have kids gently squeeze one drop of dishwashing liquid on top of the food color spots. **Watch the witnesses go!** The food coloring will instantly "spread out" and erupt into colorful swirls. Keep watching. The colors will eventually disperse throughout the cake pans.

When we put our faith in Jesus, he gives us what we need to spread the Good News to others. We have the Holy Spirit living in us, ready to take us to the ends of the earth.

Lab Results

• How should we be like the fast-acting dishwashing liquid?

• What does a "witness for Christ" mean to you?

• Name two ways you can be a witness "to the ends of the earth."

God gives us the great gift of salvation, and he wants us to help others receive the gift, too. He sent the Holy Spirit to help us do the job. Spread the news!

Something Extra!

Pour milk or water into a bowl. Take a paper clip and place it on the tines of a fork. Gently place the paper clip, as level as possible, on the surface of the liquid. Once the paper clip floats, add one drop of dish soap. Oops! Watch as the clip falls to the bottom of the dish. *(Fun Science Fact: The detergent disrupts the surface tension of the liquid.)*

You will receive power when the Holy Spirit comes on you; and you will be my witnesses in Jerusalem, and in all Judea and Samaria, and to the ends of the earth.

Acts 1:8

SUPER Science facts

The detergent breaks up the fat globules in the "resting" milk. As the globules break and expand, they create movement in the milk, allowing the food coloring to spread across the surface of the milk.

USE THIS SCIENCE ACTIVITY WITH:

• God sends the Holy Spirit. Acts 2:1–12. *(God sent the Holy Spirit to empower his followers to spread the Good News.)*

• John the Baptist. Luke 3:1–18 *(John the Baptist preached the coming kingdom of God so everyone would have a chance to be part of it.)*

• Jesus calls the disciples. Matthew 4:18–22; Luke 5:1–11; 6:12–16 *(Jesus gave the disciples the job of following him so they could be fishers of men.)*

HOP UP AND HOPE

Kids have moments when they feel hopeless. As they watch pepper hop up on spoons, they'll learn that God has a purpose for them.

Truth Explosion: Because Jesus finished the work God gave him, I can keep doing the work God gives me.

GODPRINT:
Purposefulness

TIME:
10 minutes

GROUP SIZE:
Groups of 4

MESS METER
1 2 3

Sometimes I feel hopeful. Other times I feel frustrated. How about you? Pause for kids to respond. **I agree. Sometimes it's a real tug of war between the excited and happy person that lives in here** (point to your heart) **and the grumpy and sad one that wants to move in!**

FORMULA
for success
• paper plates
• plastic spoons
• salt
• pepper
• wool sock or scarf

Let's have fun with a little "hopeful" science today. Set out one paper plate for every four students. Give each student a plastic spoon.

Go ahead and sprinkle a spoonful of "happy and hopeful" salt on your plates. Pause. **Now sprinkle a spoonful of "sad and hopeless" pepper.** Hold up the wool sock. **Rub your spoons on the sock, then slowly move your spoons across the surface of the plate. Then take a quick peek at your spoons.** The pepper should take a mighty leap onto the spoons.

Let your sad and hopeless times rise to Jesus. He'll help carry them, just as he carried the heavy, wooden cross to Calvary. No matter what the situation—daily disappointments or constant problems and worries—God has a purpose for you and wants you to do his work.

Lab Results
• When do you feel hopeful? What makes you feel sad or hopeless?

• If you know there's a good reason to do something, how does that change your attitude about doing it?

• What kind of work does God give us to do when we're young? How about when we're older?

God sent Jesus to earth to do a job—to make a way for us to know God. Now God wants us to carry on that work. No matter how we feel, God has a purpose for us. And he's ready to help! Hop up and hope—then do God's work.

Whatever you do, work at it with all your heart, as working for the Lord, not for men.

Colossians 3:23

SUPER
Science facts

Static electricity causes the salt and the pepper to be attracted to the spoon. But it is much easier for the pepper to "jump up" and stick to the spoon because it is lighter than the grains of salt.

USE THIS SCIENCE ACTIVITY WITH:

• Joseph becomes governor in Egypt. Genesis 41:1–43; 42:1–47:33 *(Joseph discovered the purpose that God had for his life.)*

• Jesus tells Peter, "Feed my sheep." John 21:1–19 *(Jesus gave Peter a job to do even after all the mistakes Peter made.)*

• Mary accepts her place in God's plan. Luke 1:26–38 *(When the angel Gabriel visited Mary, she learned the purpose that God had for her life.)*

PRAISE TO THE BRIM

A fruit drink gives your kids a picture of lives full of praise for Jesus.

GODPRINT:
Praise

TIME:
15 minutes

GROUP SIZE:
Individual

MESS METER
1 **2** 3

USE THIS SCIENCE ACTIVITY WITH:

- Triumphal Entry. Matthew 2:1; 21:1–11 *(The people praised Jesus as king.)*
- Shepherds and wise men worship Jesus. Luke 2:8–30; Matthew 2:1–12 *(Even though Jesus was a baby, the shepherds and wise men praised him as king.)*
- Mary anoints Jesus with perfume. Matthew 26:6–13 *(Mary offered the best that she had as an act of personal worship.)*

Truth Explosion: Jesus is worthy of our highest honor.

Before class, freeze cherries in ice cubes.

Even as a baby in his mother's arms, Jesus was king—king of the Jews. When he grew, the crowds greeted him as king. The last book of the Bible, Revelation, gives us a picture of heaven, where everyone will worship Jesus as the King of kings. I believe Jesus deserves our highest praises. Let's enjoy "cups of praise" in his honor and raise the praise to the brim!

FORMULA for success
- clear plastic cups
- lemon-lime soda
- ice cubes with cherries inside
- banana slices
- pineapple chunks
- melon balls or chunks
- orange juice
- trays or tablecloth to capture spills

Fill each cup half full with soda. Have kids slowly add a cherry ice cube and watch how the ice displaces the soda and the level of liquid rises. Pour in orange juice and watch the fizz rise! Finally add fruit pieces to the cups one at time and raise the level of liquid without overflowing!

Lab Results
- Your "cup of praise" just might overflow. Why would this be a good thing?
- What can we do to raise the level of praise we give to Jesus?
- Tell me why your heart brims with praise for Jesus.

Rejoice in the Lord always. I will say it again: Rejoice!

Philippians 4:4

THE PRESSURE'S ON

In 30 seconds, this activity will help your kids see they don't have to understand God's power to know that it's real.

Truth Explosion: Because we believe in God's loving power, we can ask him to help others.

Let's see if we can simulate what it's like to experience power that you can see, but don't really understand. In just a moment I'll ask you to move to a wall and stand facing it, with your toes just three to four inches from the wall. **When I say, "Press," press the backs of your wrists to the wall. Press hard, and we'll count to 30 together. Ready? Move to a wall.**

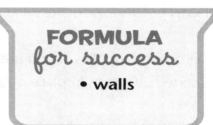

FORMULA *for success*
• walls

As you press the backs of your wrists to the wall, count slowly to 30: "One thousand one, one thousand two," etc. When you reach 30 have everyone take three steps back from the wall. As the muscle tension of pressing hard against a fixed object is released, everyone's arms will "float" upward.

Weird, isn't it? But there's a simple explanation. You've created a lot of muscle tension by pressing against the wall. Your floating arms are a result of that tension being released. When Jesus healed people or did other miracles, his power wasn't so easily explained. In fact, there's only one explanation: Jesus is the Son of God! The good news for us is that God wants us to ask him when people need his help.

Lab Results
• Why is it important to believe in God's power when we pray?

Is any one of you in trouble? He should pray.

James 5:13

GODPRINT:
Prayerfulness

TIME:
5 minutes

GROUP SIZE:
individual

MESS METER

1 2 3

USE THIS SCIENCE ACTIVITY WITH:
• The fiery furnace. Daniel 3. *(The young men maintained their belief that God would save them even in this danger.)*
• Jesus heals the nobleman's son. John 4:46–53 *(The nobleman asked Jesus for what his son needed.)*
• Jesus heals ten men with leprosy. Luke 17:11–19 *(Ten men didn't hesitate to ask Jesus for what they needed. Jesus willingly responded.)*

CONFETTI WONDERS

This shake up experiment will help kids see that it's possible to let go of hurt feelings and respond with forgiveness.

Truth Explosion: Because God forgives, I can forgive people who hurt me.

Set out the supplies. If you prefer, use zip-top bags inserted into cups in place of the jars.

GODPRINT:
Forgiveness

TIME:
10 minutes

GROUP SIZE:
Individual or small groups

MESS METER
1 **2** 3

• Have you ever had a friend you really liked—and then you had a fight?
• Why is it sometimes hard to separate the things we like and dislike about each other? (*It's easier to focus on annoying things; if someone does something hurtful, it's hard to forget and forgive.*)

FORMULA
for success
• baby food jars
• cut-out confetti (the shiny kind used to decorate party tables.)
• clean sand
• pitcher of water
• 2 tablespoons oil
• measuring cups and spoons

We need to focus on forgiving, and on seeing the good in each other—not on the bad (although that does seem easier to do!). Let's see what it takes to separate the good from the bad.

Sprinkle two teaspoons of confetti in each jar. **Let the confetti glitter represent the godly choices we make to forgive.**

Pour in two tablespoons of sand. **Sand will represent the hurts. Fill your jar with water. Let's finish the experiment by pouring in the oil and sealing the jars.**

• How do you think the "good" feelings will separate from the "bad?"

Shake your jars! As the elements are mixed, the glitter will attach itself to the oil. The sand should remain free-floating. **After a good shake, set your jar down and watch what happens.** As the jars sit, the elements will settle—the heavier sand to the bottom, the lighter oil and confetti to the top.

Lab Results

• What happened to the "good" and the "bad" in the jar?

• Do emotions have to settle before forgiveness can take place? Explain.

• How can this experiment remind you of forgiveness?

God forgives us, and he wants us to forgive others. Sometimes that's hard—okay, it's always hard!—but God's way is the only way to settle things in the end.

Bear with each other and forgive whatever grievances you may have against one another. Forgive as the Lord forgave you.

Colossians 3:13

USE THIS SCIENCE ACTIVITY WITH:

• Jacob and Esau are estranged and reconciled. Genesis 27–33 *(The brothers accepted the good and the bad in each other and mended their relationship.)*

• Joseph forgives his brothers. Genesis 37–45 *(Joseph had every reason to seek revenge, but because he saw God's purpose, he forgave his brothers for the way they treated him.)*

• David spares Saul. 1 Samuel 24:1–20 *(Saul tried several times to kill David. And David had his chance for revenge. But David respected Saul's role as king and spared his life.)*

STUFFED ON PRAYER

Use the natural curiosity found in children to help them learn to pray with confidence.

Truth Explosion: Because God listens, I can pray with confidence.

GODPRINT:
Prayerfulness

TIME:
10 minutes

GROUP SIZE:
Pairs or small groups

MESS METER

1 **2** 3

Depending on the size of your group, you may want to have kids try this activity in pairs or small groups. Demonstrate first, then let kids try.

Our Truth Explosion tells us that because God listens, we can pray with confidence. Pour an inch of water into the basin. Hold up the newspaper. **I feel confident that I can place this newspaper in the water and it will not get wet!**

FORMULA *for success*
- paper
- clear drinking cups
- shallow basin
- water

Stuff a rolled up wad of paper tightly into the jar so it won't fall out. Then set the jar (open end down) into the basin of water. If you lift the jar straight out, the newspaper will stay nice and dry.

Air is lighter than water. You can't see it, but you know it's there. It's what kept the water from the newspaper. In the same way, we can't see God, but when we pray, his presence surrounds us. We can pray confidently because God listens.

Encourage kids to take turns trying this experiment in their small groups.

Lab Results

• Name two tasks that you can perform more confidently when you ask God to help you.

• How can God's presence surrounding you help you head off temptation to do something you know is wrong?

• What is your favorite time of day to pray?

God is listening. We can talk to him about anything, anytime, anywhere. He cares about you!

Do not be anxious about anything, but in everything, by prayer and petition, with thanksgiving, present your requests to God.

Philippians 4:6

USE THIS SCIENCE ACTIVITY WITH:

• Jesus teaches his disciples how to pray. Luke 11:1–4 *(We can use Jesus' prayer as a model for our own.)*

• The church prays for Peter. Acts 12:1–17 *(God listened to Peter's friends.)*

• Daniel and the lions' den. Daniel 6:1–28 *(Thrown into the lions' den because of his prayer life, Daniel continued to pray.)*

• Elijah calls on God and God answers. 1 Kings 18:18–45 *(God answered Elijah's prayers on Mt. Carmel.)*

SUPER Science facts

Air is invisible. Yet it is made up of tiny particles that take up space. In today's experiment, the air blocks the water from entering the glass. But...if you could push your glass deep enough (into a lake, pond, or ocean) the water pressure would eventually allow water to seep into the glass and wet the newspaper.

PEACE AND CARROTS

With some simple items from the kitchen, your kids will get a picture of the resurrection power of God. In it we find peace for life eternal with him in heaven.

Truth Explosion: God's resurrection power is greater than anything we can imagine.

GODPRINT:
Hope

TIME:
10 minutes

GROUP SIZE:
Large or small groups

MESS METER

1 2 3

FORMULA
for success
- glass of water
- salt
- sliced carrot piece
- teaspoon

When you watch old cartoons, you see characters get smashed over the head with huge boulders or run over by a freight train. They're flattened for a moment then they pop right up and run off again. But we all know that's not what happens in real life. We're careful about a lot of the things we do because we know that if we get hurt that badly, we could even die. And life is too precious to be careless.

Fill a glass with water. **What do you think will happen if we drop a piece of carrot in this water?** *(It will sink.)* Ask a volunteer to drop a piece of a carrot into the water and watch it sink.

• Is there anything we can do to make that carrot come back up? Jiggle the glass? Blow on the water?

We might say that this carrot has had it. It's not coming back to life, so to speak, no matter how hard we wish it would. We have no power to change it. There's nothing we can do.

But God's power is greater than human power! In the Bible, God's power accomplished amazing things including raising people from the dead. Imagine! Let's say this salt represents God's power.

Ask a volunteer, or several, to add salt to the water a teaspoon at a time. The carrot will suddenly rise to the surface.

We can celebrate God's resurrection power in our lives. It gives us peace of mind to know that God's will for our lives is eternal life with him in heaven.

Lab Results

- Tell me three words that describe God's power.
- Why is it important to know that God's power is greater than human power?
- What does "resurrection power" mean to you?

If God can raise the dead, then surely he can solve our problems. This same power is at work in our lives. God can do great things.

Where, O death, is your victory? Where, O death, is your sting?

1 Corinthians 15:55

Something Extra!

Drop a peeled orange into a pitcher of water. What happens? It sinks. Try it again with the whole orange. Yes! It rises.

USE THIS SCIENCE ACTIVITY WITH:

- Jesus raises Lazarus. John 11:1–44 *(With resurrection power, Jesus brought a family hope where there was none.)*

- God raises Jesus from the dead. *(God showed his resurrection power in victory over death and in salvation for us.)*

- God's power raises the Shunamite boy. 2 Kings 4:8–33 *(God answered Elisha's prayers with resurrection power. God answers our prayers with the same power.)*

SUPER Science facts

The carrot is lighter than the denser or heavier salt water, causing it to rise and sit on the water's surface.

CAN'T POP MY JOY

Find the inner joy of knowing Jesus.

Truth Explosion: Because God showed his love by sending Jesus, I can worship him as my Savior.

GODPRINT:
Joy

TIME:
10–20 minutes

GROUP SIZE:
Individual

MESS METER

1 2 3

Before class, stretch out two light-colored balloons. Use the rubber end of a pencil to push one balloon inside the other, leaving the lip of the internal balloon extended. Fully blow up the outer balloon. Pinch the ends and hold the balloons up to the light. (You should see the inner balloon resting limply inside the other.) Finally, blow up the inner balloon half as full as the outer one. You'll need lip and cheek muscles to push the air through! One knot will close both balloons. Blow up two or three balloon-in-balloon pairs and drop them inside a bag.

When you're ready to begin class, grab the bag of balloons and set it close to you. Don't forget to thread a sewing needle into your sleeve cuff. Pass out new balloons to your kids. Ask students to blow them up and pinch them shut with their fingers. Do not knot. Make sure to blow up a balloon for yourself.

• What kind of feelings could balloons represent?

We might say that balloons represent the way we feel when we have no joy or excitement in our hearts. We feel deflated as if the air swooshed right out of us. Release your balloon and let kids to do the same. Watch as balloons zip through the room and fall.

Take a "balloon-within-a-balloon" from the bag by your side and hold it high for kids to see. **Here's another balloon, and it represents something** completely different. Joy! A joy so strong, nothing can pop it! Remove the needle from your sleeve and prick the top of the outer balloon. **Pop!** Still, your kids will be surprised to see the fully intact balloon inside! Use your extra balloons if the trick doesn't work the first time.

Joy is knowing that all year long the Son of God lives inside of you. No matter what happens on the outside, you can have joy on the inside. If you have time and supplies let kids prepare their own double balloons and practice popping the outer one.

Something Extra!

This experiment can be done in reverse, but it's a lot trickier. Grab a small and a large balloon. Follow the instructions above but knot the smaller, internal balloon and push it *inside* the larger balloon. (The inner balloon should float freely inside.) Then blow up the larger balloon half full. Squeeze the smaller balloon against the knotted part of the outer balloon. Press your needle into the side of the outer balloon (where the balloons touch) just enough to leave an indentation. Pop! The inner balloon should pop, leaving the outer balloon intact.

Lab Results

- Show me with your face what you feel like on the inside when you're joyful.
- How do we show our joy when we worship?
- How is joy different from happiness?

We might think that a lot of things make us happy at least for the moment. But true joy can bubble up even when we're having hard times. Recognize the joy that comes from Jesus living inside you!

The LORD is my strength and my shield; my heart trusts in him, and I am helped. My heart leaps for joy and I will give thanks to him in song.

Psalm 28:7

USE THIS SCIENCE ACTIVITY WITH:

- Birth of Jesus. Luke 2:1–20 *(The angels and shepherds were joyful at the birth of Jesus.)*
- Resurrection joy of Easter. John 20:1–18 *(The news that Jesus was alive brought intense joy.)*
- Nicodemus meets Jesus. John 3:1–21 *(Jesus introduced Nicodemus to the joy that comes from being born again.)*

SUPER Science facts

The amount of air in a filled balloon determines the flexibility of its skin and its ability to withstand pressure. A hole or break in the balloon's skin is a point of weakness which causes a rapid tear and, thus, an overall surface failure.

BAG O'TRUST

Would you trust a bag with a hole in it? Use this activity to show kids that God is 100% trustworthy.

Truth Explosion: Because God has helped his people in the past, I can trust him with my future.

GODPRINT:
Conviction

TIME:
10 minutes

GROUP SIZE:
Large group or small groups

MESS METER
1 **2** 3

Pick up your zip-top bag of water and the sharpened pencil you brought to class. Choose an amiable student and hold the bag over his or her head. Place the sharpened pencil point perilously close to the bag!

Trust. Trust is something that grows right alongside love. Babies trust their mothers. Children trust their parents. And students, of course, trust their teacher! Walk around the classroom pausing now and then to hold the water-filled bag above more heads. As you do, ask the following questions:

- Can you tell if someone is truly trustworthy? How?
  - If you were to write a book titled, "Trust: Pass or Fail," what chapter titles would it include?

> **FORMULA**
> *for success*
> - zip-top bag of water
> - sharpened pencil
> - Optional: candle, match, balloon

Set out a large basin or have kids join you at the sink or take a short trip to the water fountain. If you have extra sharpened pencils bring them along. **I need a head, any head. You can trust me!** Have your brave volunteer place his or her head over the sink. Place the bag over his or her trusting head. Look for a wrinkle-free bulge in the bag. With a twisting motion, push the sharpened pencil point into the bag until you break the surface. There should be no major leaks. Continue to twist until the pencil pokes out the other side. **I told you I could be trusted. A nice, dry head!** Leave the pencil in place. Have kids use extra pencils and bags to give this a try.

Helpful Hint: Pull out pencils *only* if you wish bags to drain.

I'm grateful that you trust me. Thank you. But trust can fail miserably in human hands. Feelings like anger, jealousy and greed will leave us disappointed and upset. But our loving God is 100% trustworthy. And because God has helped people in the past, we can trust him for what's coming up.

Something Extra!

Fill the bag 1/4 full of water. Place over a candle's flame. Will it break, spewing water all over the place? No! *(Fun Science Fact: The heat moves into the water so quickly that the polymer membrane of the bag will not burn.)*

Lab Results

• Name a Bible story that shows God's care.

• Tell about a time God took care of you in your past.

• What things in your future would you like to trust God to take care of?

Whatever happens, the same God who has been with his people in the past will be with us in the future. Trust him!

Do not fear, for I am with you; do not be dismayed, for I am your God. I will strengthen you and help you; I will uphold you with my righteous right hand.

Isaiah 41:10

USE THIS SCIENCE ACTIVITY WITH:

• God leads his people out of slavery in Egypt. Exodus 6:1–12:32 *(Moses trusted God and served as leader of the people with the conviction that God was in control.)*

• Josiah repairs the temple and finds God's Word. 1 Kings 22:1–23:30 *(King Josiah discovered God's Word in the temple and led the people back to following God's way.)*

• Stephen preaches and dies for the faith. Acts 7:1–60 *(Stephen preached about God and accepted death.)*

SUPER Science facts

The zip-top bag is made of a chemical compound known as a polymer. When the bag is pierced, the plastic (made of long chains of molecular units) closes around the object, sealing it closed.

THE EYES HAVE IT

Discover with your kids that we don't always see what's right in front of our faces!

Truth Explosion: God wants us to have eyes of faith and let him work in our lives.

GODPRINT:
Confidence

TIME:
10–15 minutes

GROUP SIZE:
Individual or pairs

MESS METER

1 2 3

FORMULA *for success*
- white paper
- markers
- rulers

Each eye has what's known as a "blind spot." It's true! In the very back of our eyeballs, is a part called the retina. The retina is made of light-sensitive material that sends information it sees to the brain. Every retina has a "blind spot," or a place that doesn't have that light-sensitive material.

Let's find our blind spots. There are a couple of tricks we can do to find them. Give each child a piece of white paper and a black marker. **Turn your paper so it's long, not tall. Now, on the left-hand side, about two inches from the edge and near the middle of the page, draw a black dot about the size of a pea.** Help the kids do this. **Measure six to eight inches to the right of that dot and draw a small plus sign (+).**

When your kids are ready, say, **Close your right eye. Now hold the paper about 20 inches away from your face.** (You may wish to have the kids work in pairs. One can hold the paper while the other does the experiment, then they can switch.) **With your left eye only, look at the plus sign. Got it? Now very slowly, bring the paper closer to your face. Keep looking only at the plus sign.** The plus sign will suddenly disappear. **Oops, where did it go? Right! The plus sign has fallen on the "blind spot" of your retina!**

If you wish, have kids repeat the experiment but this time close their left eyes.

Here's another blind-spot experiment your kids can try.

Draw two horizontal blue lines side by side with a gap of about 1/4 inch between them. About one inch to the right of the second bar, draw a red dot. Ask kids to close their right eyes and look at the red dot with their left eyes. Again, hold the paper about 20 inches away from the face and bring it close. What happens? *(At a certain distance, the blue line will appear unbroken.)*

• Jesus rises and appears to Thomas. John 19:1–18; 20:1–8, 19–31 *(When he saw the proof for himself, Thomas had new confidence that Jesus was alive; Jesus said that those who believe without seeing are blessed.)*

• Bartimaeus believes Jesus will heal him. Luke 18:35–43 *(Bartimaeus was confident that Jesus could heal him and was determined to ask.)*

• Jesus heals a blind man. John 9:1–11 *(Jesus performed a miracle so that the people could be confident in his Father's power.)*

Want more? Draw a smiley face on the left part of a sheet of paper like this.

  9 8 7 6 5 4 3 2 1

On the right edge, place the number one and count up to nine, writing right to left. Close right eyes and look at the number one with left eyes. See the smiley face with your peripheral vision! Without moving heads or papers, look at the other numbers (the 2, then the 3, then 4, etc.) What happens? *(The smiley face should disappear around the four and reappear around the 7.)*

Lab Results

• What do you think it means to have eyes of faith?

May the God of hope fill you with all joy and peace as you trust in him, so that you may overflow with hope by the power of the Holy Spirit.

Romans 15:13

SUPER *Science facts*

In these experiments, the brain receives different messages from the right and left eye. Doing the best it can in interpreting what it sees, the brain combines the two images.

A DIME ON THE BALL

Kids discover that even good hearts are heavy with sin.

GODPRINT:
Commitment

TIME:
10 minutes

GROUP SIZE:
Pairs or groups

MESS METER

1 2 3

USE THIS SCIENCE ACTIVITY WITH:

- God calls Moses to lead his people. Exodus 3:1–4:17 (At first, Moses wasn't sure he was the right person for the job, but he stuck with it and got the job done.)
- Esther saves God's people. Esther 1–9 (Esther could have kept her Jewish identity a secret, but she was determined to do God's will instead.)
- Saul is converted. Acts 9:1–28, 13:1–3 (We can show our commitment to God by sharing God's message the way Paul did and expecting that God will change people.)

Truth Explosion: We can stay committed to God even though we're sinful.

Place the cookie sheet at your feet. **People hurt one another. Unfortunately, such hearts are heavy with hate and selfishness.**

Hold up the dime. **The dime represents a hateful heart. It's small and not of much value.** Hold up the baseball. **Let's say this baseball is a pretty good heart, large and easy to hold.** Hold the dime in one hand and the baseball in the other. Extend both hands in front of you. **Watch!** Open your hands and let both objects fall onto the cookie sheet. Both items hit the cookie sheet at the same time.

This can't be right! Here, you try it. Hand the ball and dime to a student and witness the same result. **It seems no matter what state our hearts are in—pretty good, mostly good, a little bad, or terribly hateful—each of us has a sinful heart and is in need of Christ's forgiveness. Let's commit our lives to Christ and became a new creation in him.** Kids can kneel, sit, stand, or, with supervision, drop objects from a window.

Lab Results

- What must you do to have a changed heart and new life in Christ? (*Confess wrong doings; give my life to Christ.*)
- How do you know if your changed heart is the real thing? (*It leads to a new life in relationship with Christ.*)

> **If anyone is in Christ, he is a new creation; the old has gone, the new has come!**
>
> 2 Corinthians 5:17

FORMULA *for success*

- baseballs
- dimes
- cookie sheet

A HOLE-Y HAND

All you need is a simple piece of paper for this lesson on hope.

Truth Explosion: We can give others the hope God gives us.

Distribute the paper. **On one half of your paper color a design that communicates feelings of hopelessness. For the other half, pick color choices that best express positive, hopeful feelings.**

> **FORMULA**
> *for success*
> • 8 1/2 x 11 paper
> • markers

Demonstrate how to roll the paper into a tube shape. Have your kids do the same. **Now hold your tube up to your eye.** Demonstrate the action for your kids. **Now hold your other hand up next to the tube near the top**

like this. Your kids will see a "hole" in the palm of their hands. **Pretty amazing but not nearly as amazing as what Jesus does for us when we feel discouraged!** The "hole" vanishes when the paper is lowered.

Lab Results
• What helps you go from feeling hopeless to hopeful?
• How does Jesus use his power to give you hope?
• What things can you do that will help other people feel hopeful?

For you have been my hope, O Sovereign LORD, my confidence since my youth.

Psalm 71:5

GODPRINT:
Hope

TIME:
5 minutes

GROUP SIZE:
Individual

MESS METER
1 2 3

USE THIS SCIENCE ACTIVITY WITH:

• Jesus raises Jairus's daughter from the dead. Luke 8:40-42, 49-56 *(Jesus gave hope when everyone thought it was too late.)*

• Jesus calms the storm when the disciples are afraid. Mark 4:35–41 *(Jesus reminded the disciples of his power.)*

• Jesus raises Lazarus from the dead. John 11:1–44 *(Jesus restored hope to the family and friends of Lazarus.)*

• God promises a son to Abraham. Genesis 15:2–6; 17:15–17; 21:1–6 *(God gave Abraham a hope that seemed impossible—a son in his old age.)*

A NICKEL FOR YOUR THOUGHTS

Kids will rise to the challenge of plunking a nickel in a cup with a few rules that open the door to talking about submitting to God's authority.

GODPRINT:
Submissiveness

TIME:
10 minutes

GROUP SIZE:
Large group or small group

MESS METER
1 2 3

Truth Explosion: Jesus shows us how to put ourselves under God's authority to do his will.

Life is full of hard challenges. I have one to start our time together. And I'll need your help. Place the drinking glass on the table and cover it with the index card. Place the nickel in the center of the index card.

FORMULA
for success
- drinking glass
- nickel
- index card
- Optional: checkers

Now here's the hard part and where I'll need your help. How can I get this nickel to fall into the cup without changing the nickel's position on the index card or touching the card with my fingertips? Listen as your kids offer suggestions. **No, Chris, you cannot touch the nickel. No, Justin, you cannot lift the card.**

Applaud the student who offers the following solution: Use two fingers to snap or flick the card from the top of the glass. The card should shoot forward away from the cup—and kerplunk! —the heavier coin, which does not move as quickly, will drop into the drinking glass.

Lab Results
- How did you feel about the rules to this little experiment?
- How did the rules work in our favor once we figured out the trick?
- God tells us how he wants us to live. How does that work in our favor?

Like the nickel on the index card, we're stuck in the middle of this great big world. And that means having to do hard things, difficult things—things we feel we just can't do. But God's strength gets us moving in the right direction.

Something Extra!

The same principle of inertia applies to the following activity. Make a stack of ten checkers. Place an additional checker near the base and flick it, aiming for the bottom checker. The bottom checker should shoot out from the stack, leaving the tower neatly standing.

We know that we have come to know him if we obey his commands.

1 John 2:3

SUPER Science facts

At the beginning of the experiment both the card and the nickel are in a resting or motionless state (known as inertia). When the card is flicked, gravity pulls the "resting" coin into the cup.

USE THIS SCIENCE ACTIVITY WITH:

- Ten Commandments. Exodus 20:1–21. *(God tells us how we can please him by living in submission to him.)*

- Jesus submits to God's will in the Garden. John 17:1–18:11 *(Jesus accepted God's plan.)*

- Joseph accepts his role in God's plan. Matthew 1:18–2:15 *(Joseph could have walked away from Mary, but he accepts the role God chose for him.)*

CHEMICOOL!

Love is a basic life need and the very nature of God. As this chemical experiment grows it will show your kids how to grow and grow in love.

GODPRINT:
Love

TIME:
20 minutes to begin forming

GROUP SIZE:
Large group

MESS METER

1 **2** 3

Truth Explosion: Because God shows us the meaning of love, we can love other people.

If you cannot find laundry bluing to perform this experiment, it can be done without it. The result, however, will not be as striking.

Place the briquettes in a bowl. **Let's say these charcoal briquettes are my six little buddies. Who will give my buddies a hand?**

Have kids glue wiggly eyes on the briquettes.

My buddies seem a pretty close group. They sit in the same school bus every morning. They see each other in class just about every day and they eat cheeseburgers in the cafeteria at lunchtime. But...because my buddies don't take the time to know one another they can't ever become devoted, caring friends. Let's change that!

FORMULA
for success

- 6 charcoal briquettes
- shallow bowl
- salt
- laundry bluing (look in the laundry section of your store or ask your grocer)
- water
- ammonia
- food coloring
- tablespoons
- Optional: wiggle eyes, glue

• What would be a great way to start a conversation with someone new?
• How can a soccer team on the playground show a newcomer that he or she belongs?

When my buddies see how much they have in common, a loving friendship is sure to grow. Let's see our buddies grow in love!

Have kids mix six tablespoons of salt, six tablespoons of laundry bluing, six table-spoons of water and one tablespoon of ammonia and spoon it over the bri-quettes. Also drop some colorful food coloring on top of each of the briquettes. Wait. In twenty minutes or so, small crystals will begin to form on the charcoal. (Beware: This experiment is an assault on the nose. In other words, it stinks! But the end product is well worth it.) On Day 2 be sure to sprinkle on more salt.

Lab Results

• Explain what happened in our little chemistry experiment.

• Why are kids afraid to reach out in friendship to someone new? How can a group of loving friends change that?

Love is patient, love is kind. It does not envy.

1 Corinthians 13:4

SUPER Science facts

As the water evaporates on the charcoal surfaces, deposits of solids are left behind, forming crystals. Crystals are also formed as the solution is drawn up into the porous charcoal, a process known as capillary action.

USE THIS SCIENCE ACTIVITY WITH:

• The gift of love. 1 Corinthians 13 (We can look to God, the author of love to help us love others.)

• Prodigal Son. Luke 15:11–32 (God loves us no matter what we do.)

• Wise/Foolish builders (In the context of loving others and not judging). Matthew 7:1–21; 24–27 (We can treat other people with love and build our house on the rock of God's foundation.)

• Jesus' birth. Luke 2:1–20. (We receive God's love when we receive the gift of his Son.)

MOVE IT

Move a brick with pencils? Kids will enjoy the wonder of physics as they try this simple experiment on strength.

GODPRINT:

Perseverance

TIME:

15 minutes

GROUP SIZE:

Large or small groups

MESS METER

1 2 3

Truth Explosion: God gives us strength.

Gather everyone around a brick, flat stone or other heavy object that has a fairly flat bottom. Try to choose something that the kids will not be able to move easily on their own. Let the kids take turns trying to push the stone along the floor or ground. (If you have a large class, you may want several sets of supplies.)

Show the pencils to your class. **Can you think of a way these pencils can make the job easier?** Pause to let kids speculate. Then have kids place one pencil every few inches under the heavy object and try again to move it. This time it will roll! Have the kids "keep up" with the moving object, continually placing pencils under the object so it moves uninterrupted across the floor.

FORMULA
for success

- large bricks, flat stones or books
- round pencils, new crayons or other cylindrical objects
- Optional: balloon, penny

Every day we face situations that seem overwhelming. We think we can't fix the problem or get the job done. When we trust God to show the way, he gives us the strength we need.

Lab Results

• How did using the pencils help make the job of moving the brick easier? *(The pencils carried the weight of the brick, and their shape helped keep it moving.)*

• Tell about something you had to do recently that was really hard.

• When you feel like giving up, what helps you to keep going?

...ace situations that seem overwhelming and just too hard, ...to remember that God gives us strength to hold on.

Finally, be strong in the Lord and in his mighty power.

Ephesians 6:10

Something Extra!

For another quick lesson on perseverance, push a penny inside a balloon. With the penny resting at the bottom of the balloon, blow up the balloon. Shake the balloon to get the penny moving in a circle. The coin will roll a long time on the smooth interior surface.

SUPER Science facts

When items rub or press against each other it causes resistance or friction. Depending on the surfaces this can speed or slow down moving objects. For example, rolling produces less friction than sliding.

USE THIS SCIENCE ACTIVITY WITH:

- Ruth and Naomi trust God. Ruth 1–4 (Ruth and Naomi had a lot of reasons to give up, but they kept on going.)

- Solomon builds the temple. 1 Kings 5–8 (God gave Solomon the job to build the temple. Solomon got the job done with excellence.)

- Nehemiah rebuilds the wall of Jerusalem. Nehemiah 4–7 (Nehemiah ran into a lot of obstacles, but kept performing the job God gave him to do.)

- Esther saves God's people. Esther 1–9 (Esther planned carefully and persevered to save God's people.)

- Paul is a prisoner and shipwrecked. Acts 27:1–28:10 (When the whole ship and crew were in danger, Paul persevered and gave encouragement.)

JARS OF FORGIVENESS

Watch as even the darkest mistakes disappear in this picture of God's forgiveness.

GODPRINT:
Forgiveness

TIME:
10 minutes

GROUP SIZE:
Small or large group

MESS METER
1 **2** 3

Truth Explosion: Because God is forgiving, I can serve him even when I make mistakes.

God's forgiveness can take care of all our mistakes, big and small. Let's see how God's forgiveness gives us a clean slate so we can keep on serving. As you do this experiment, keep in mind that bleach will discolor carpet and clothes. Cover rugs and table tops with plastic, and wipe up any spills right away. Also take precautions so bleach does not come into contact with skin or eyes.

FORMULA
for success
- baby food jars
- water
- eyedropper
- dark-colored food coloring
- liquid bleach

Have kids fill the jars with water. **Let's begin by putting one drop of food coloring into the water. See how just a drop colors every part of the water?**

Put a few more drops of food coloring into the jar. Use an eyedropper to put a drop of bleach into each cup. Your kids will be amazed to watch the dye slowly disappear. Continue to add bleach until the water is clear. **This is a simple experiment you can do with your family. Don't forget the cleansing power of God's forgiveness!** Make sure to dispose of the bleach and water solution as soon as the experiment is completed.

Lab Results
- How does the food coloring remind you of what sin does in our lives?
- How is the bleach like what God does for us?

Even when we make mistakes, God forgives us and gives us a fresh start. He wants us to keep on serving him even though we're far from

ur sins, he is faithful and just and will forgive us our sins and purify us from all unrighteousness.

1 John 1:9

SUPER Science facts

Bleach contains a chemical known as sodium hypochloride. When the oxygen in the hypochloride releases, it combines with chemicals in the dyes to create a colorless solution.

USE THIS SCIENCE ACTIVITY WITH:

- Jesus tells Peter, "Feed my sheep." John 18:15–18, 25–27; 21:1–19 (*Even though Peter had denied Jesus, Jesus forgave him and gave him a job to do.*)

- Zacchaeus finds forgiveness. Luke 19:1–10 (*Zacchaeus accepted Jesus' forgiveness and wanted to make up for what he had done wrong.*)

- Jesus forgives the thief on the cross. Luke 23:38–43 (*God can forgive anyone, at any time.*)

- Saul is converted and becomes Paul, the missionary. Acts 9:1–22 (*God forgave someone who hated his own Son and his people.*)

START YOUR ENGINES

The race doesn't always go to the swift, but to one who keeps a loyal pace with the Savior of the world.

Truth Explosion: Jesus is our leader; we can follow him.

GODPRINT:
Loyalty

TIME:
20 minutes

GROUP SIZE:
Pairs or groups

MESS METER
1 **2** 3

It may seem that the best runners win the race every time. But in Jesus' eyes, it's not the speed at which you follow him that matters, just that you do! There's a first-place prize—eternal life!—for everyone who crosses the finish line and remains loyal to Jesus.

FORMULA
for success
- two empty jars (the same size)
- water
- 3-ring binder
- masking tape
- circle stickers
- permanent markers

Hand the jars and markers to two volunteers and ask them to make a smiley face expression on each of the jars—two eyes, a nose and a curved smile. **Meet Jim and Jake!** (Or substitute names of your choice.) **Jim's been running all day. He's pretty thirsty.** Fill one of the jars with water and screw on the lid. **Jake likes walking. He's not quite as thirsty as Jake.** Place a few drops of water in jar two. Secure the lid.

Place the three-ring binder on the floor. Adhere a masking tape "finish line" two feet away. Now lay both jars on their sides and get ready to roll them from the top of the binder "ramp."

- Who will speed down the ramp first?
- Who will cross the finish line first?

Jim or Jake? Who will it be! Release the jars. Surprisingly, "Jim" (the water-the bottom of the ramp first, but "Jake" (the air-filled jar) ___ first. Have your kids give the experiment a try. If you ___ in the empty jar a little at a time to see "Jake's" reaction. ___ hem finish at the same time.

Lab Re___

a Danny Price ___

- What does loyalty mean to you? Have you had a friend who wasn't loyal?
- Why is it important to have your eyes on the prize each day?
- Who can you turn to when you feel like giving up the race and going your own way?

Jesus is our leader. When we are loyal, we follow him wherever he leads us.

Do you not know that in a race all the runners run, but only one gets the prize? Run in such a way as to get the prize.

1 Corinthians 9:24

USE THIS SCIENCE ACTIVITY WITH:

- Jesus calls the 12. Matthew 4:18–22; Luke 5:1–11; 6:12–16 *(The disciples chose to be part of Jesus' group and to be loyal to him.)*

- God chooses a king for his people. 1 Samuel 16:1–3; 2 Samuel 5:4; 7:11–13 *(We continue to be loyal to the kingdom that continued through David's line in Jesus.)*

- Stephen preaches. Acts 7:1–60 *(Stephen's loyalty in the face of death demonstrated his unshakable faith that God was and is in control.)*

SUPER *Science facts*

The weight of a water-filled jar is evenly distributed relative to its volume. This results in increased speed and the jar rolls down the ramp faster. Yet, on a flat surface the water-filled jar's weight causes friction (between the jar and the floor), slowing it down. The lighter jar takes the prize.

POP CHOICES

Easy does it! Put a wooden skewer in a balloon without popping it as a reminder not to pop off when things aren't fair.

GODPRINT:
Self-control

TIME:
15 minutes

GROUP SIZE:
Individual

MESS METER
1 **2** 3

Truth Explosion: We honor God when we control our selfish impulses and make wise choices.

Set out the materials listed. Have kids stretch balloons and blow them half full.

Things happen to us that aren't fair. But that doesn't mean we have to "pop off!" It's the harder choice but the right one. Draw or write a few words on your balloon about an unfair event or situation that might cause you to pop off, then tell a partner about it. Pause as kids work.

FORMULA
for success
- balloons
- markers
- pointy wooden skewers
- cooking oil

Because God is fair and just, we can trust him to make things come out right. God can help us develop thick skin so we don't pop off, but choose careful responses. Have kids brainstorm trusting, positive responses to the situations printed on their balloons.

Coat a skewer with oil. Using a gentle twisting motion, push the skewer through the "dark circle" (the thickest part of the balloon) on top. The balloon shouldn't pop. Demonstrate, then let kids try their own balloons. Give extra balloons to kids who want to try this with their families.

Lab Results
- What kept the balloon from popping? *(Careful work; going slow; self-control.)*
- Why is it sometimes hard to control ourselves when we want to pop off?

• What will help you remember to make good choices the next time you're tempted to pop off?

Pretty good, huh! When we control our own impulses when things are unfair, we honor God with our actions and attitudes. Self-control takes the prize every time—the gratitude and love of God our Father.

I have learned the secret of being content in any and every situation.

Philippians 4:12

SUPER Science facts

Balloons are made of thin sheets of rubber latex. These intertwined strands of polymer molecules can easily stretch around the skewer because of the flexibility of the polymer chains.

USE THIS SCIENCE ACTIVITY WITH:

• Adam and Eve choose to disobey God. Genesis 3:1–24 *(Adam and Eve failed to control their choices and suffered the consequences.)*

• Joseph is put in prison unfairly. Genesis 39–40 *(Joseph demonstrated self-control and patience when he was treated unfairly.)*

• David shows self-control and spares Saul. 1 Samuel 26 *(David could have taken Saul's life to get back at him, but he showed self-control and did the right thing instead.)*

• Martha thinks Mary is unfair. Luke 10:38–42 *(Martha lost her self-control, and Jesus gently reminded her of what's important in life.)*

WATER'S UPS AND DOWNS

With this experiment your kids discover that confidence is on the rise when they least expect it.

Truth Explosion: God gives us his promises; we can be confident.

GODPRINT:
Confidence

TIME:
20 minutes

GROUP SIZE:
Large group

MESS METER
1 **2** 3

If your class is large, you may want to set up more than one station for observation or repeat the experiment. Everyone needs the opportunity to observe close up.

Before class use a couple drops of melted wax to stick one candle to each pie tin and make enough reproducible handouts for your class.

Let's perform this experiment and see how our confidence in God can rise when we trust in his awesome power.

Fill the first tin with one-half-inch of water. Add a few drops of blue food coloring for a water look. Set a glass over one of the unlit candles. **Fill in the "I saw" space on your handout with a description of the set up we have here.** Give your class a few seconds to observe and write.

Fill the second tin with one-half-inch of water. Drop in some food coloring. **I'm going to light this candle and set a glass over it. What will happen? Fill in the "I Predict" space on the handout.**

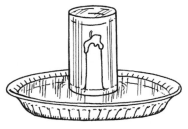
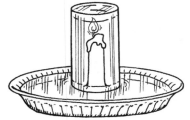

- How sure are you that you know what will happen?
- What makes you really sure about something?

Now watch carefully. Light candle #2. Place the glass over the candle. The candle will extinguish and the water will rise inside the glass.

Just like the water in our experiment, our confidence rises when we believe God's promises. Solve the code on your sheet to find out what happened to the water—and our confidence.

Something Extra!

If you wish, try this simple experiment as well. Fill a balloon half full with water. Knot closed. With your lit candle in place, hold the water-filled balloon directly in the candle's flame. Your kids are sure to think that it will pop. The balloon's bottom will blacken but it won't burn! Water has amazing heat-holding properties and will absorb and distribute heat quickly—without bursting the balloon.

Lab Results

- Can you think of a time when you need to depend on God's promises?
- God can do things that we don't expect. How do you feel about that?
- Name a situation this week where you will depend on God's promises.

Trust God's promises because God tells us they're true. That gives us all the confidence we need, no matter what ups and downs we face.

Though an army besiege me, my heart will not fear; though war break out against me, even then will I be confident.

Psalm 27:3

USE THIS SCIENCE ACTIVITY WITH:

- Noah and the ark. Genesis 6–9. *(Despite what other people thought, Noah was confident that God had a plan.)*
- Daniel in the lions' den. Daniel 6:1–28 *(Daniel was so confident in the true God that he continued to pray even though his life was in danger.)*
- Three friends in the fiery furnace. Daniel 3:1–30 *(The friends are confident that they serve the one true God and he will take care of them.)*
- Elijah on Mt. Carmel. 1 Kings 18:16–39. *(Elijah was confident that he was calling on the true God, not the false god, Baal.)*

Water's Ups and Downs

Watch the water carefully during both parts of this experiment.

What happens to the water when you put a glass over an unlit candle?

I saw:

_____

_____

_____

_____ .

What do you think will happen to the water when you put a glass over the lit candle?

I predict:

_____

_____

_____

_____ .

HOW DOES THIS WORK?

The candle burns all the oxygen. Hot air escapes. Pressure from the outside air makes room for more water in the glass.

Spaces:

```
 __  __  __  __  __  __  __  __  __  __    __  __  __  __  __
  5  17  15  14   6   8  11  15   5  11     7   6  10  11  10

 __  __  __  __    __  __    __  __  __  __  __  __  __
 13   3  11  15    13  11     2  11   9   6  11  18  11
             ,
 __  __  __  __    __  __  __  __  __  __  __  __ .
 16  17   8  10     4   7  17  12   6  10  11  10
```

KEY:

2	B
3	H
4	P
5	C
6	I
7	R
8	D
9	L
10	S
11	E
12	M
13	W
14	F
15	N
16	G
17	O
18	V

[Answer: Confidence rises when we believe God's promises.]

KINDNESS CALENDAR

Kindness has long-lasting effects that stick where you least expect.

Truth Explosion: Jesus shows us how to be kind to people with needs.

Gather enough supplies for each group of three or four kids to have a set. Ask kids to break up into small groups and settle down around the containers and other items you've set out. Be sure to make photocopies of the Kindness Calendar handout for the kids in your class.

Who has a kindness calendar at home? No? I believe everyone should have something that reminds him or her to show kindness to others. When kindness becomes hard for others to see in us, Christ's love is hidden. People may need help yet we are blind to their needs.

• What needs pop up at school or on the way to school that you might miss because you're too busy talking and having fun with your friends?

FORMULA
for success

• copies of Kindness Calendar from p. 101
• pencils
• white glue
• liquid starch
• food coloring
• measuring cups
• mixing spoons and disposable plastic containers
• disposable wipes for smudged fingers

GODPRINT:
Kindness

TIME:
20 minutes

GROUP SIZE:
Small groups

MESS METER

1 2 **3**

Pass out copies of the Kindness Calendar and pencils. **Here's a kindness calendar to get you started. Pick one of the spots on the calendar and jot down one small and simple way you can show kindness that day. Use as few words as possible. This will help when we make the fun "kindness putty" experiment for today.**

- Jesus heals an official's son. John 4:46–53 (*Jesus responded with kindness when he heard of an official's son's illness.*)

- Jesus heals Bartimaeus's blindness. Mark 10:46–52 (*Jesus kindly stopped his journey and sought out Bartimaeus to find out what he needed.*)

- Jesus feeds 5,000 people. John 6:5–14 (*Jesus could have sent the people away, but instead he took action to meet their needs.*)

- Jesus heals a shriveled hand. Matthew 12:9–14 (*Jesus gave priority to the man with a need rather than to the rules of the Sabbath.*)

Once kids finish writing have them put the pencils and papers aside. Have groups divvy up duties: pick a "Glue Guru," a "Color Extraordinaire" and a "Starch Archer."

For each group, measure one cup of white glue and put it in a plastic container. Add a few drops of food coloring and stir. While stirring continually, slowly pour in one cup of liquid starch. Keep stirring until the mixture holds together. Touch it. If it feels sticky, stir in a bit more starch until the mixture forms a smooth, rubbery consistency. Now pull and stretch to see how the kindness putty works.

Tear off a piece of putty and press it onto the words you printed on your paper. Pause. **Slowly lift the putty.** The penciled words will adhere to the putty, albeit backwards! **Kindness really sticks, doesn't it?** Have kids fill in more spaces on the calendar and try the putty again. Pass out the wipes to clean fingertips and hands.

Lab Results

- Why do we sometimes miss the hurts and struggles of others?
- When can we "open our eyes" and become more sensitive to the needs of others rather than thinking of all the things we want?
- Think of Bible stories that showed the world the kindness Jesus had for people he did not know at all.

Jesus gives us an example of kindness. He saw people's needs and decided to help. That's the wonder of kindness!

Be kind and compassionate to one another.
Ephesians 4:32

Kindness Calendar

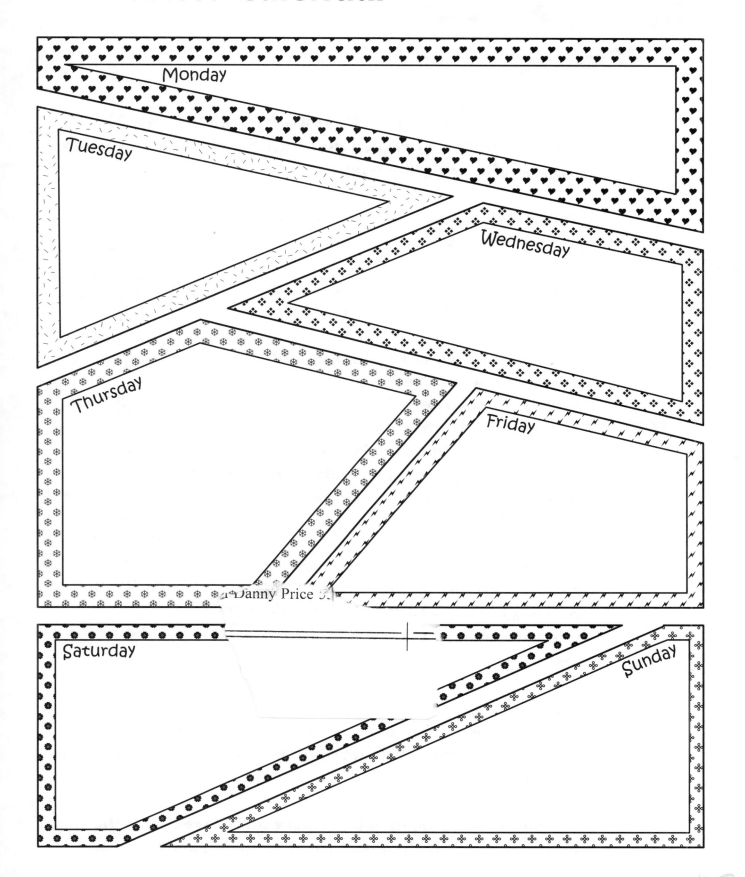

Monday

Tuesday

Wednesday

Thursday

Friday

Danny Price

Saturday

Sunday

WHIRLIGIG FAIR

Kids always want what's fair—in their minds. This paper windmill project gives kids a chance to reflect on the choices they make.

Truth Explosion: We're responsible for the choices we make.

GODPRINT:
Fairness

TIME:
20 minutes

GROUP SIZE:
Individual

MESS METER
1 2 3

Before class, make copies of the Pick a Patch Whirligig reproducible for your kids.

God created each of us with free will. That means we're free to make our own choices, for good or for bad. Sometimes we have to suffer the consequences of a bad choice. And that's fair in God's eyes even if it doesn't feel good. Allow the Holy Spirit to help you make choices that please him.

Give kids the Pick a Patch Whirligig handout and encourage them to fill in the three choice corners with thoughtful statements about their parents. Explain that they'll need Mom or Dad to complete the last choice corner.

FORMULA
for success
• copies of Pick a Patch Whirligig from p. 104
• pencils
• markers
• scissors
• push pins
• new pencils
• Optional:
• glitter glue
• tacky glue or glue sticks
• fabric scraps
• blow dryer to quick-dry the glue

Then invite kids to use lots of imagination and the fun things you've provided to decorate the patterned triangles. They may want to color the designs in a starburst motif, highlight them with glitter glue, or cover them with paper or fabric patches.

Cut out the Whirligig square and make cuts where they're shown on the handout. Fold each corner toward the middle and stick a push pin

through the center and into the top of the eraser of a new pencil. Roll the pencil back and forth between your hands and see how the pattern you created animates.

As kids work, encourage them to talk about their families. Ask about their parents' interests, their siblings, their rooms, and what they really like about their families. Have kids plan a good time such as supper or bedtime to share these projects with their parents.

Lab Results

• Are you always happy with the choices your parents make for you? Why?

• Are you always happy with the choices you make for yourself? Explain.

• Sometimes our choices affect other people. How can we be fair or unfair in the choices we make?

Give me understanding, and I will keep your law and obey it with all my heart.

Psalm 119:34

SUPER
Science facts

Air is an invisible force. The folds in the paper whirligig catch the moving air (wind) and make it spin. A steady wind of 3 to 5 miles per hour will keep your whirligig in constant motion.

USE THIS SCIENCE ACTIVITY WITH:

• Adam and Eve choose to disobey God. Genesis 3:1–24 *(God was fair when he allowed Adam and Eve to suffer the consequences of their choices.)*

• Abigail keeps David from revenge. 1 Samuel 25:1–35 *(Abigail's husband did not do what was fair, and David almost responded with a poor choice. Abigail helped him do what was right.)*

• David spares Saul's life. 1 Samuel 26:1–25 *(It would have been "fair" for David to exact revenge on Saul, but David chose God's way instead.)*

Pick a Patch Whirlygig

Draw or write to complete statements 1, 2 and 3. Then create starburst color schemes in the patterned triangles or cover the triangles with patches of light fabric or paper. Cut out the square on the solid line. Make the diagonal cuts shown in the pattern. Fold the starred corners to the middle and stick a push pin through the center and into the top of a pencil eraser. Roll the pencil back and forth between your hands and see how the pattern you created animates. Take your whirlygig home and ask Mom or Dad to fill out the last triangle.

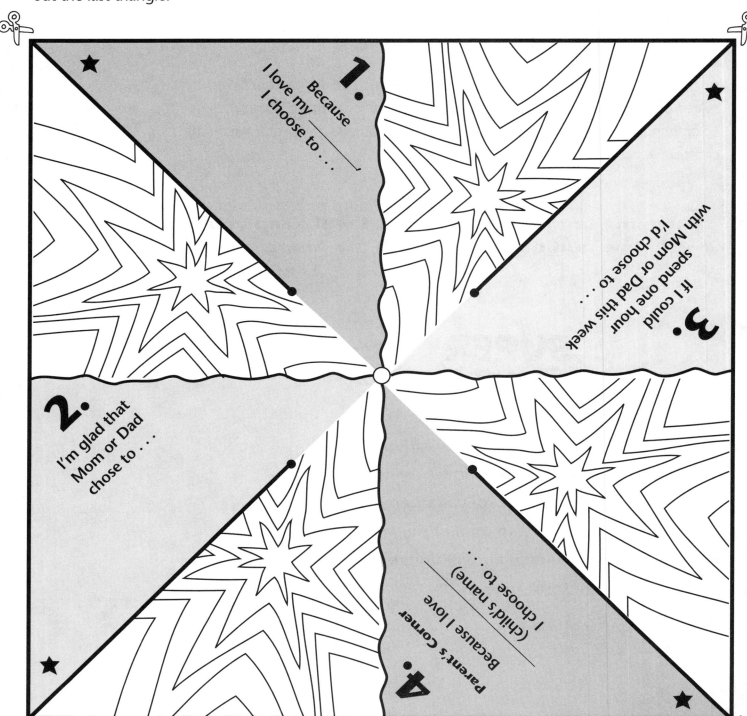

1.
Because
I love my _____,
I choose to . . .

3.
If I could
spend one hour
with Mom or Dad this week
I'd choose to . . .

2.
I'm glad that
Mom or Dad
chose to . . .

4.
Parent's Corner
Because I love
_____ (child's name)
I choose to . . .

INVISIBLE COMMANDMENTS

We honor God when we control our human impulses and follow his commandments.

Truth Explosion: Because God tells me how to treat others, I honor him in my relationships.

Before class, make copies of the Invisible Commandments handout.

Did you know that Jesus summed up the Ten Commandments in two simple statements? We can find them in Matthew 22:36–40. Find the passage in the Bible with your kids and have a volunteer read it aloud. **Let's transform Jesus' words into a secret message.**

Set out cups with lemon juice. Pass out copies. Have students place their papers in front of them. In pencil, have kids fill in the "Dear _____" line at the top left, then sign their names at the bottom right. Show them how to remove excess cotton from the swab tip, then dip the swabs into lemon juice and write "Love God!" on their papers. Be sure they use enough juice to see each letter. The juice will dry in about 10 minutes.

Once the paper dries, it will look blank. To read the secret message, supervise children carefully as they pass the paper back and forth over a candle's flame or a 100-watt light bulb.

Have the kids roll their papers, tie them with colorful ribbon or raffia and take

GODPRINT:
Self-control

TIME:
20 minutes

GROUP SIZE:
Individual

MESS METER

1 2 3

FORMULA
for success

- Bibles/pencils
- paper cups
- lemon juice
- cotton swabs
- copies of Invisible Commandments from p. 107
- 6-inch pieces of ribbon or raffia
- candle and match or lamp with 100-watt bulb
- Optional: hand-made or decorative paper or crumpled brown paper

- God gives the Ten Commandments. Exodus 19:1–8, 20:1–21 *(God gave his people the guidelines for self-control.)*

- Religious leaders question Jesus. Matthew 22:36–40 *(Religious leaders tried to play question games with Jesus about the commandments.)*

- Parable of the Good Samaritan. Luke 10:25–37 *(The people who passed the injured man had an opportunity to show they understood the commandments. Only the Samaritan showed the self-control needed to respond to another's needs.)*

them home. Encourage kids to ask their parents, "Do you know how Jesus summarized the Ten Commandments?"

Optional: If you wish, have kids cut out the tablet shape from the handout and glue it to brown bags that have been crumpled then smoothed out for a stone-like effect.

Lab Results

- What does it mean to love the Lord with all your heart, soul and mind?
- Who did Jesus mean by "your neighbor"?
- How do these statements of Jesus sum up the Ten Commandments?

God tells us how he wants us to treat others. When we do what he says, we honor him in our relationships. The invisible commandments become visible because they're written on our lives!

Love the LORD your God with all your heart and with all your soul and with all your strength.

Deuteronomy 6:5

Something Extra!

Soak pieces of red cabbage in a bowl of water. Wait 30 minutes. In a measuring cup, place a 1/2 cup of lemon juice (an acid) followed by a splash of the cabbage liquid. Watch as purple turns red—instantly!

Invisible Commandments

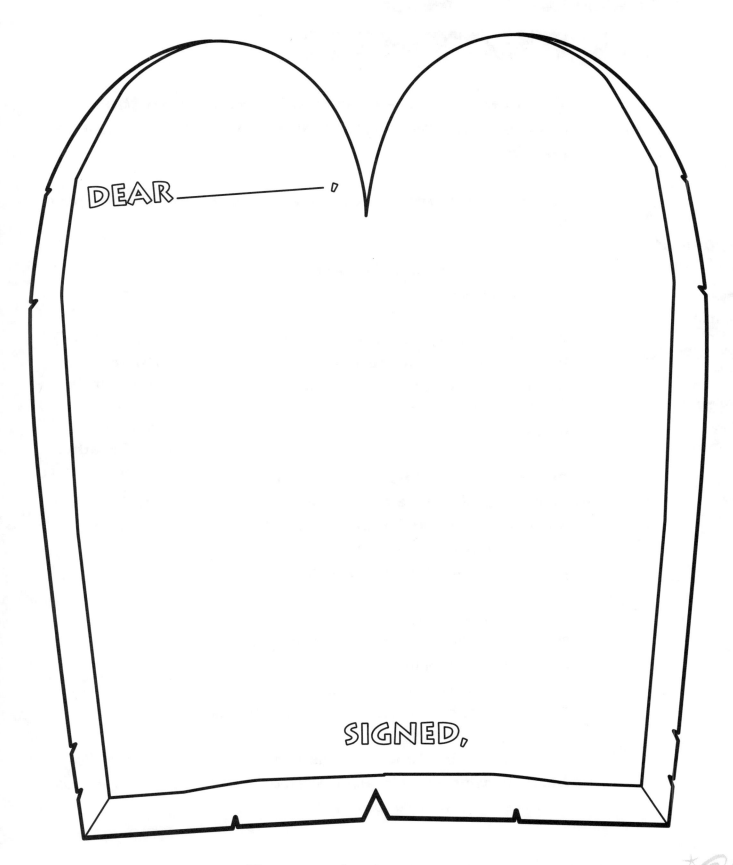

DEAR————,

SIGNED,

HEAVY AS A FEATHER

This crafty science project will remind kids that because they belong to a powerful God, they can be confident.

Truth Explosion: God can do amazing things; we don't have to be afraid.

GODPRINT:
Confidence

TIME:
20 minutes

GROUP SIZE:
Individual

MESS METER

1 2 3

Before class, make copies of the Feather Lander Landing Pad handout.

God did amazing things for his people in the Bible. Let's name some of the stories of God's amazing work. Pause for kids to name some of their favorite Bible stories.

Our God is amazing! He's more powerful than any problem we could have. Let's make a Feather Lander craft that will surprise you—and help you share with your families God's good miracles.

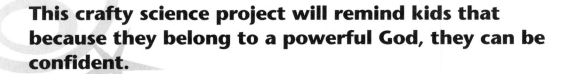

FORMULA
for success
- round washers
- colorful feathers
- rubber bands
- 4-inch fabric squares
- copies of Feather Lander Landing Pad from page 110

To make Feather Landers:
Place a washer in the center of the fabric square.
Pull up the corners of the cloth.
Push 3 or 4 feathers in the top opening.
Tightly bind the cloth and feathers with a rubber band.

Toss your Feather Lander several times and see if you can discover what's amazing about it. *(Fun Science Fact: Because of the weight of the washer, the feather lander will land upright just about every time!)*

Give each child a Feather Lander Landing Pad. Have them partner up and take turns trying to hit each of the sections of the page with their Feather Landers and then do what the target says. Encourage them to play again at home with their families.

Lab Results

• What's amazing about your Feather Lander? *(It lands upright every time)*

• How does this remind you of how powerful God is?

• How will remembering God's power help you be more confident the next time you have a big problem?

God is powerful, and we belong to him. We don't have to do anything on our own. We always have God's presence and help.

The LORD himself goes before you and will be with you; he will never leave you nor forsake you. Do not be afraid; do not be discouraged.

Deuteronomy 31:8

USE THIS SCIENCE ACTIVITY WITH:

• God brings plagues on Egypt and frees the Israelites. Exodus 6:1–12:32 *(Despite a rough start, Moses gained confidence as he confronted Pharaoh and led the people out of Egypt.)*

• Joshua obeys God and conquers Jericho. Joshua 6:1–20 *(Despite some very strange instructions, Joshua was confident in God's leading as the people conquered the Promised Land.)*

• Gideon and 300 men defeat the Midianites. Judges 7:1–8, 16–21 *(God took away human overconfidence when he asked Gideon to go into battle with just 300 men.)*

• An angel frees Peter from prison. Acts 12:5–17 *(The people prayed confidently for Peter's release.)*

Tell about a time when God did something amazing for you.

Tell about a time when you were afraid until God helped.

The LORD himself will go ahead of you. He will be with you. He will never leave you. Deuteronomy 31:8

Tell about something you can do without being afraid because you know God is with you.

Tell about a time when God did something amazing for someone you know.

WAX THANKFUL

"Please" and "Thank you" are wonderful to hear from any child.

Truth Explosion: God gives me what I need; I can be thankful.

Before class, make copies of the I Can Thank God handout.

It's fun to surprise someone with a thank you card. When we do, we're doing what God wants us to do. Let's make surprise wax pictures and thank our Creator!

Pass out the reproducible. Ask kids to use a white candle to color in the large letters that say *I Can Thank God*. **Now, paint over the entire page with dark watercolor paints. The letters will show through despite the paint!** Trim pictures with lace or ribbon.

Lab Results
- When is it easy to be thankful?
- Why is it sometimes hard to be thankful?
- Why is it important to be thankful even when things aren't going your way?

God gives us what we need. We can trust him to take care of us, and we can be thankful for his love and care no matter what happens.

Give thanks in all circumstances, for this is God's will for you in Christ Jesus.

1 Thessalonians 5:18

FORMULA for success
- white candles
- white paper
- copies of I Can Thank God from page 112
- dark watercolor paints
- paintbrushes
- lace or ribbon trim
- glue
- scissors

GODPRINT:
Thankfulness

TIME:
20 minutes

GROUP SIZE:
Individual

MESS METER
1 **2** 3

USE THIS SCIENCE ACTIVITY WITH:

- Jesus heals 10 men with leprosy. Luke 17:11–17 *(Jesus healed 10 men, but only one remembered to thank him.)*

- The Lord is our shepherd. Psalm 23 *(God gives us everything we need; we can depend on him and respond with thanksgiving.)*

- Hannah is thankful and gives her son to God. 1 Samuel 1:1–2:11 *(Hannah prayed for a son and God provided. In thankfulness, she gave her son to God's service.)*

Wax Thankful

CROWN SURPRISE

Make paper crowns that hold a unique twist as a reminder that we can trust God in scary situations.

Truth Explosion: We can call on God and know that he will respond.

Scary situations make us feel alone and uncared for. Let's make a reminder that when we call on God, the king of the universe, he always hears us. Pass out copies of the Crown Surprise handout.

Cut out the flat crown you see on the paper. Then fold in the jewel tabs on the dotted lines. Crease them extra hard and push them flat against the crown.

As kids work, set out cookie sheets and pour enough water in each one to just cover the bottom. Ask kids to gather round with their folded crowns. **Now gently lay your paper crowns on the water and watch.** Wait a minute or so. (*Fun Science Fact: As the water rises inside the plant fibers of the paper, the paper swells and the tips of the crown will slowly open.*) Pluck the crowns out of the water as soon as they open. Only the bottom will feel slightly damp! Kids can take their crowns home to use as a pattern and try again.

Lab Results
• Why do we sometimes forget to ask for God's help in scary situations?
• What will this surprise paper crown help you remember?

But I call to God, and the Lord saves me.

Psalm 55:16

FORMULA
for success
• copies of Crown Surprise from p.114 on plain paper
• cookie sheets
• water

GODPRINT:
Prayerfulness

TIME:
10 minutes

GROUP SIZE:
Individual

MESS METER
1 **2** 3

USE THIS SCIENCE ACTIVITY WITH:

• Hezekiah faces battle. 2 Chronicles 32:1–23 (*King Hezekiah faced a battle he was sure to lose. God sent an angel to conquer the enemy.*)

• Daniel in the lions' den. Daniel 6:1–28 (*Daniel prayed even though he knew he might be punished. God kept him safe.*)

• Jonah prayed inside the fish. Jonah 1–4 (*Jonah repented of his disobedience and called on God for help.*)

Crown Surprise

Cut out the crown and fold the jewels in toward the center. Then set the crown in a small amount of water and watch what happens.

God hears our prayers; I can trust him in scary situations.

HEART OF THE MATTER

Capture kids' curiosity and keep them guessing as they examine the heart of the matter.

Truth Explosion: God wants us to look on the inside the way he does.

Before class, make photocopies of the Heart of the Matter reproducible. Also, cut small samples of six of the following and place on a plate: orange peel, Styrofoam®, tree bark, soap, crayons, dry skin, fingernails, chalk, chocolate candy, crushed pretzels, cotton balls, peeling paint, fish scales, shredded paper towel, hair, plant leaves or lint.

Give each person a copy of the reproducible. **God sees what's in our hearts. Let's practice looking into the heart of things to see what they're made of. Use a magnifying glass to check out what's on these plates. Write down your observations and guesses on your "Heart of the Matter" sheet.** Allow time for students to inspect the scrapings and fill out their sheets. Share findings to see if students' educated guesses were correct!

Lab Results
• What can you tell by looking at the hearts of people that you can't tell by looking at the outside?
• How can you see other people the way that God sees them?
• What would you like God to see in your heart?

...The LORD does not look at the things man looks at. Man looks at the outward appearance, but the LORD looks at the heart.

1 Samuel 16:7

FORMULA for success
• copies of Heart of the Matter from p. 116
• magnifying glasses
• paper
• pencils
• paper plates
• scrapings or samples from assorted items

GODPRINT:
Preciousness

TIME:
20 minutes

GROUP SIZE:
Individual

MESS METER
1 2 3

USE THIS SCIENCE ACTIVITY WITH:

• God chooses David to be king. 1 Samuel 16:1–13 (David was precious to God and God had a plan for him; we are all precious to God.)

• Jesus meets the Samaritan woman at the well. John 4:1–26 (Even though the Samaritan woman was a social outcast, Jesus cared enough to talk to her about living water.)

• Jesus' love changes Zacchaeus. Luke 19:1–10 (Jesus showed that even the worst sinners are precious to his Father.)

Heart of the Matter

Can you look at part of something and guess what the whole thing is? Make your observations in each box, then make a guess about what each item really is.

**God looks on the heart;
I can see others through God's eyes.**

What I See:

Color_____
Shape _____
Texture_____

I think I'm looking at the
heart of a _____.

What I See:

Color_____
Shape _____
Texture_____

I think I'm looking at the
heart of a _____.

What I See:

Color_____
Shape _____
Texture_____

I think I'm looking at the
heart of a _____.

What I See:

Color_____
Shape _____
Texture_____

I think I'm looking at the
heart of a _____.

What I See:

Color_____
Shape _____
Texture_____

I think I'm looking at the
heart of a _____.

What I See:

Color_____
Shape _____
Texture_____

I think I'm looking at the
heart of a _____.

TWIRLIBIRD

A simple paper Twirlibird will remind your kids to trust the power and wisdom of the Son of God.

Truth Explosion: Because Jesus is the Son of God, I can trust him.

Before class, make copies of the Twirlibird handout.

Wouldn't it be incredible to do amazing things? Fly? Trampoline into outer space? As we know from our Bible, our Savior didn't need to imagine amazing things. He *did* amazing things. When in doubt, remember to trust in Jesus, the Son of God. No matter what the weather—stormy, sunny or cloudy with a chance of rain—Jesus' power is timeless. Let's read the handout and fill in the blanks. Brainstorm possible situations with your kids. Jot them down on the handouts.

Cut the Twirlibird from the handout. Add a paper clip to the base of the flyer and hold it up high. Let it go! Watch as it twirls to the ground.

If you have access to a balcony or other elevated area, take your kids there to see their Twirlibirds really fly. *(Fun Science Fact: The air pressure under the Twirilibird wings gives it lift, slowing its fall to the ground. The more air under the wings, the faster it will spin.)*

Lab Results

• Why it is important to always, *always* trust in God?

Do not let your hearts be troubled. Trust in God; trust also in me.

John 14:1

FORMULA *for success*
• copies of Twirlibird handout from p. 118
• scissors
• pencils
• paper clips

GODPRINT:
Trust

TIME:
15 minutes

GROUP SIZE:
Individual

MESS METER
1 2 3

USE THIS SCIENCE ACTIVITY WITH:

• Jesus walks on water. Matthew 14:23–33 *(Peter walked on water to Jesus and learned a lesson in trust.)*

• Jesus calms the storm. Matthew 4:35–41 *(The disciples were terrified and called on Jesus to save them.)*

• Transfiguration. Matthew 18:1–8 *(At his transfiguration, some of Jesus' disciples understood that he was the Son of God and they could trust him.)*

Twirlibird

Complete the sentences on the handout. Then cut it out on the solid lines and fold on the dashed lines. Add a small paper clip to the base of your Twirlibird. To watch it twirl, hold the paper clip between your fingers and toss it high in the air.

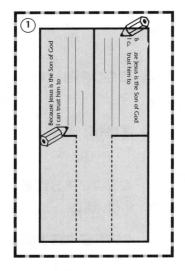

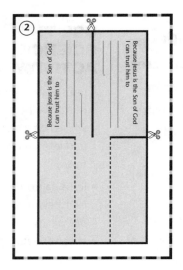

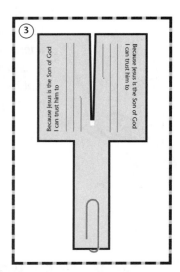

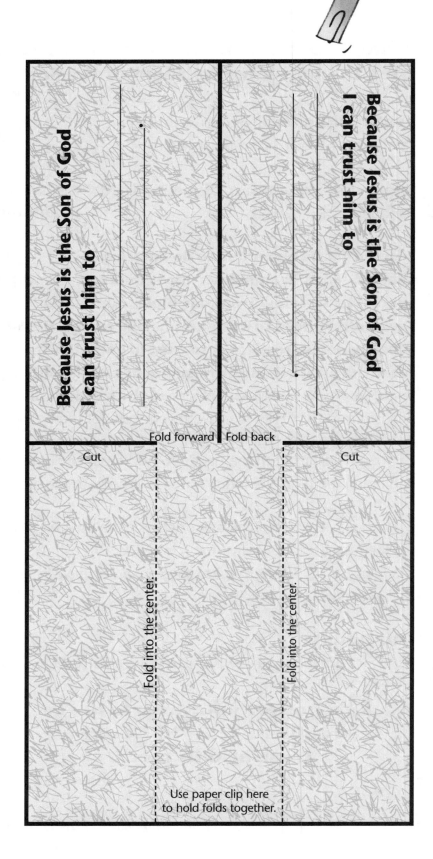

INDEX
of Scripture References

INDEX
of Godprints and Topics